A Bold Experiment:
The Charles Street
Universalist Meeting House

Exterior of the Charles Street Universalist Meeting House

Photo: Robert F. Murphy

A Bold Experiment:
The Charles Street
Universalist Meeting House

Maryell Cleary, Editor

Dedicated to the memory of
CLINTON LEE SCOTT
and
KENNETH LEO PATTON
Pioneers of a Religion for One World

ISBN: 0-9702479-3-1

Cover photo: Robert F. Murphy
Design and layout: Laura Horton

Table of Contents

Section IV: Last Things

Preface

Ernest Cassara

Nineteen hundred and forty-nine was a notable year in the history of liberal religion in the United States, the year that Dr. Clinton Lee Scott, Superintendent of the Massachusetts Universalist Convention, succeeded in bringing Universalism back to Boston. Unlike Unitarianism, which survived in a few churches, due to the changing demographics of the city the several Universalist congregations had dwindled and disbanded. Dr. Scott managed to purchase a meetinghouse on Charles Street, and the Convention called a minister to lead a liberal revival.

The ministry of Kenneth L. Patton was revolutionary. As the building was remodeled for a new beginning, the pews were arranged in the round, so that congregants faced each other, the minister no longer elevated above the worshipers. The wall of what had been the chancel eventually displayed a striking representation of the Great Nebula in Andromeda, the twin of the Milky Way Nebula. Although Patton was a forthright Humanist, a bookcase held the scriptures of the many religions of humanity. On panels on the two sides of the Nebula, and along the balconies, were placed sixty-five symbols of those religions.

It is not that religious liberals had not been concerned with the religions of the world previously. Spurred by his interest in Transcendentalism, the prominent Unitarian minister James Freeman Clarke had published *Ten Great Religions* in 1871. In the same period, a collection of the scriptures of the world's faiths became available in English translation. But, now, a church was organized that sought inspiration from sources beyond the

Jewish and Christian scriptures and traditions. The result was an expanded view of Universalism.

In addition to his radical restructuring of the setting for worship, Patton purchased a printing press. He and members of the congregation established the Meeting House Press, setting type and doing the other things connected with publishing then. (This was obviously long before the ease with which computers allow for publishing today.) From the press came materials for use in the church's services, and books and pamphlets that presented to the world Patton's vision of religion.

The Charles Street Universalist Meeting House had a profound impact on the Universalist denomination, and, in the days before the merger, of the American Unitarian Association and the Universalist Church of America in 1961, on the Unitarians as well. In this book, Maryell Cleary has brought together contributions from those who had been part of the grand experiment on Charles Street and from persons who came under the influence of Kenneth Patton and whose lives as a result were changed.

As a member of the faculty of Tufts University, I came to know Ken Patton when he traveled to Medford to preach at chapel services of the Crane Theological School and on my visits to the Meeting House. I can testify to the truth of observation of some of the contributors to this book that he possessed an abrasive personality. He certainly was not the warm, cuddly type of minister preferred by many congregations. Inspired by Chaucer's observation regarding "God's plenty," I disregarded his irascibility, with the thought that, indeed, it does take all kinds—even in the ministry. Although I did not attend services at Charles Street often, I realize now that I came under the influence of Ken's larger view of Universalism as much as the contributors to this book, who came to know him more intimately. Indeed, the entire Unitarian Universalist denomination came under his influence. When one considers the continuing influence of Patton's writings and the number of his hymns and readings in *Singing the Living Tradition*, the current denominational hymn book, it is clear his ideas live on in the liberal religious movement.

With the passage of more than fifty years since the arrival of Kenneth Patton at Charles Street, this collection provides us a provocative retrospective.

Acknowledgments

This book had its genesis in a suggestion by Robert Murphy. He reminded me that 1999 would mark the fiftieth anniversary of the founding of the Charles Street Universalist Meeting House. Both of us felt that there should be some recognition of that event. Ernest Cassara suggested that the Unitarian Universalist Historical Society's annual seminar at Harvard might be a suitable venue for a talk on the Meeting House. Peter Lee Scott, son of Clinton Lee Scott, the originator of the Meeting House, was the natural choice to give that talk.

Then the possibility of a program at the Unitarian Universalist Association's General Assembly in Salt Lake City, Utah appeared, when Charles Howe suggested that the Murray Grove Association had an extra program slot. Ellen Chulak, Murray Grove director, graciously offered it to us. Paul Sawyer, minister of Throop Memorial Unitarian Universalist Church in Pasadena, California, who had been active in the Meeting House as a young man, agreed to join Peter as a presenter. The Historical Society provided some funding to make these two events happen.

The next step was to get something into print. I was fortunate to be able to find people who had either been active in the Meeting House or had become interested in it later who were willing to write papers to add to those by Peter and Paul. Their papers, along with three by Kenneth L. Patton, whose writings lend depth and life to the collection, make up this book. Without all those who wrote or phoned or e-mailed, of course there would have been no book. So thanks, all!

Clarise Patton, her father's literary executor, kindly gave me permission to use any of his work. I appreciate her cooperation deeply. Some other individuals helped along the way: John Hurley, UUA archivist, found materials on the Meeting House for me; Howard Box sent me a collection of Meeting House sermons, among which was "The Prostitution of the Clergy," which you will find here; and Alan Seaburg, who sent me a copy of "The Future of Universalism," an address given by Ken Patton to the New York State Convention of Universalists in 1985. At every step, Ernest Cassara, a distinguished historian, actively assisted in more ways than I can tell.

Many thanks to Marty Brown, office manager at the Unitarian Universalist Church of Greater Lansing, my home church, for her work at the computer, and to the church for permission to use the church computer. Thanks also to the *UU World,* successor to the *Universalist Leader,* for permission to reprint "Art and Symbols for a Universal Religion," and to *The Proceedings of the Unitarian Universalist Historical Society* for permission to reprint Charles Howe's "He Lives Tomorrow: Clinton Lee Scott, Revitalizer of Universalism." Thanks also to the Unitarian Universalist Historical Society for permission to reprint the article on Kenneth Patton which appears in the on-line *Dictionary of Unitarian Universalist Biography,* edited by Dr. Peter Hughes. Special thanks to skilled proofreader Faith Grover Scott, ably assisted by Peter Lee Scott, and to my son, Bruce M. Cleary, by profession an editional consultant, for their professional assistance.

Grants from the Unitarian Universalist Historical Society, the New York State Convention of Universalists, and an anonymous donor made publication possible.

It took many people to make this book, not least those not named here who encouraged me and told me that this was an important work. Without their encouraging words, I might well have given up any number of times. My thanks to all of you!

—Maryell Cleary

Introduction:
Why This Book

Maryell Cleary

At the midpoint of the twentieth century something startling happened in the small world of liberal religion. In, of all places, the conservative Massachusetts Universalist Convention. It bought a church building in Boston, hired a radical minister from the Midwest and gave him free rein to create a broader Universalism than there had ever been before.

Such excitement in the beginning! Such innovative ideas, such inclusion of all the arts and all the world's religions! It began in 1949, this Charles Street Universalist Meeting House, flourished for a time, caused great controversy in staid old Massachusetts, then dwindled, and finally went into the dustbin in 1980. Today few people remember this bold experiment.

This book is the story of that experiment as told by some of the participants, by the minister, and by others who looked at it from the outside and even from the distance of years. As an experiment supported financially, though meagerly, by a denominational body, it was and is unique. Those who participated fully found it exciting and inspiring. Those who saw it as radical condemned it and sought to end financial support. Even its minister, Kenneth L. Patton, said towards the end of his life that he didn't know whether the Meeting House was the best thing he'd ever done, or the worst.

I have a large bump of curiosity. I saw the Meeting House only once, and not for a service. I wanted to know what it was really like for those who participated. And I wanted to let others know what it was about. It is a part of liberal religious history, and its story is fascinating: both wonderful and sad. It has things to say to us in a new century, a new millennium.

Section I

Background, Personae, Controversy

Chapter 1

The Charles Street Meeting House:
An Unfinished Dream

David Bumbaugh

To appreciate fully the importance of the Charles Street Meeting House and the vision it embodied, it is essential that the experiment be placed in the context of Universalist history in North America. Only within that context is it possible to understand the truly radical nature of this undertaking and the remarkable consequences of the effort.

Although there had been a tendency toward universalism among the German Brethren in Pennsylvania as early as the first quarter of the eighteenth century, the Universalist movement had its organizational beginnings in Massachusetts toward the end of that century. Throughout most of its history, Universalism's greatest strength would be found in Massachusetts and New York. Indeed, while denominational headquarters were in Boston, by 1870 there were more Universalists in New York State than any other state in the Union.

Sweeping out of their strongholds in New York and Massachusetts, nineteenth-century Universalists carried their evangelical gospel west, establishing churches in cities and small towns all along the frontier. So effective were their efforts that for a while it seemed to some that Universalism might become the dominant faith of much of the nation.

One source called Universalism "the reigning heresy of the day." Another source credited the Universalists with more than six hundred thousand adherents. Yet another named it as the sixth largest denomination in the country.

Universalist statistics never supported these extreme claims. Nonetheless, beginning from nothing, Universalism did exhibit phenomenal growth in the first decades of its existence. However, whatever the actual numbers may have been, by 1860, the movement was no longer growing faster than the population of the country, and the high-water mark may have been reached by 1870 when Universalists celebrated the centennial of their movement. Then followed a period of stagnation and gradual decline that, after the First World War, steepened dramatically.

Over the years, a number of explanations for this failure have been put forward. Many have blamed the decline of Universalism on inadequate organizational support for such rapid growth. Others have suggested that Universalism was the victim of demographic changes which eroded the rural and small-town base of the movement. Still others have suggested that Universalism succeeded in ameliorating the emphasis on eternal punishment in the theology of main-line Protestantism, thus obscuring the distinction between Universalism and other religious alternatives. The history of the movement after 1870 suggests that Universalists themselves sensed that the failure resulted from a combination of organizational problems and of a lack of clarity about the central message of the movement and its relation to the rest of Protestant Christianity.

After the organizational restructuring that occurred in 1870, Universalists sought to define the movement more clearly and to introduce greater discipline into the faith structures of the movement. The new constitution affirmed the Christian basis of the movement and dropped the traditional freedom clause which had allowed room for a modicum of diversity of theological opinion. Subsequently, Universalists tried Herman Bisbee of Minnesota for heresy and stripped him of his ministerial fellowship. For the next twenty years, Universalists debated virtually every element of their faith, until, exhausted, they resolved the matter by reinstituting the freedom clause. They entered the twentieth century, focused, as were many Protestants, upon the Social Gospel movement, and borrowed much of their language and program from other religious bodies, especially the Methodists.

By the mid-1920s Universalists were forced to confront a decline that had avalanched into crisis. Some saw the source of the problem in the drift of the movement from its Christian roots. Others, reflecting on the Universalist experience with its missionaries in Japan, began to suspect that Universalism might have a message that was broader than Christianity. In the last decade of the nineteenth century, a Universalist mission to Japan had confronted the need to explain the Universalist gospel to a culture that had never embraced the concept of eternal punishment in hell. This raised questions about whether Universalism was only a corrective of Protestant teachings concerning hell or whether it might have a larger message which was significant beyond the boundaries of Christian thought. In 1893, the World Parliament of Religions meeting in Chicago brought Universalists into direct conversation with a variety of religious opinions, once more raising the question of whether Universalism was only a variant of Protestant Christianity or whether it could be part of a large religious conversation.

Several factors conspired to undercut the arguments of those who defined Universalism as part of the larger Protestant Christian movement. In 1933, the appearance of the *Humanist Manifesto* challenged traditional religious assumptions. Of the signers of the Manifesto, only one, Clinton Lee Scott, was a Universalist minister, though two other signers, Charles Francis Potter and J.A.C. Fagginer-Auer, held joint ministerial fellowship with the Unitarian and the Universalist denominations. Most Universalists were not supportive of the Manifesto with its call for a this-worldly, reason-based, nontheistic, nonsupernatural religion. However, the appearance of the *Manifesto* demonstrated anew the need for Universalists to restate their message to a changed and changing world.

In 1935, the General Convention, meeting in Washington, DC, adopted, with little debate or controversy, a new "Bond of Fellowship and Statement of Faith." The statement was a remarkable departure from previous statements. It reflected a new Christology—Jesus as a leader, a spiritual model, his relation to God left unspecified. It reflected a changed eschatology—gone was the concern about life after death; instead the

Kingdom of God was seen as the earthly consequence of ongoing human effort. The Bible was not mentioned and God was defined in impersonal terms—as "eternal and all-conquering Love." By 1935, if Universalism had not yet fully departed from Christianity, it had opened the door to a much broader understanding of its mission.

The man who walked through that door was Robert Cummins. Elected General Superintendent in 1938, Cummins set about to revitalize a demoralized movement suffering from decades of decline. At his suggestion, the General Convention of Universalists became the Universalist Church of America in 1942, and its delegate body came to be known as the General Assembly. Addressing the Assembly the following year Cummins said:

> Universalism cannot be limited either to Protestantism or to Christianity, not without denying its very name. Ours is a world fellowship, not just a Christian sect. For so long as Universalism is universalism and not partialism, the fellowship bearing its name must succeed in making it unmistakably clear that all are welcome: theist and humanist, unitarian and trinitarian, colored and colorless. A circumscribed Universalism is unthinkable.

Cummins was not yet speaking for all Universalists. Many were still deeply committed to their Christian heritage. But his message was given added impetus by the reaction of the larger Christian community. In 1942 and again in 1944, the Universalist Church of America sought admission to the Federal Council of Churches. On both occasions it was rejected on theological grounds: the Council determined that Universalists were insufficiently Christian since they did not condition membership upon an affirmation of Jesus Christ as Lord and Savior.

From 1946 through 1954 a group of young ministers calling themselves "The Humiliati" sought to renew the denomination by encouraging a "universalized Universalism." Critics suggested that there was nothing humble about any of these recent graduates of Crane Theological School. Nevertheless, their discussions provoked renewed reflection on the content of the Universalist gospel and the relation of Universalism to the larger religious culture. Out of their deliberations emerged a new symbol for Universalism—a cross off-center in a circle, intended to demonstrate that while Universalism had emerged from the Christian tradition, Christianity was not longer central to the Universalist gospel. Those who took offense at this graphic representation of the New Universalism were given another cause for alarm when one of the Humiliati refused to be ordained to the Christian ministry and insisted instead on being ordained to the Universalist ministry.

It was in the context of this groping toward a New Universalism that the Massachusetts State Convention in 1949 under the leadership of its Superintendent, Clinton Lee Scott, established a new congregation in Boston—the Charles Street Meeting House—and called the Rev. Kenneth L. Patton to be its minister.

Subsequent events demonstrate that everyone understood, at some level, what was at stake in this venture—that the Charles Street Meeting House was intended to be a substantial break with the past and an effort to incarnate a radical vision of the future. Its supporters justified the existence of the Meeting House on the basis that it was time for "a liberal church in Boston." The Meeting House was intended to offer an alternative to the "tradition-bound" Unitarian churches in the city. Its opponents delayed its admission to fellowship in the Massachusetts Convention precisely because they understood that the Meeting House challenged the conventional assumptions and practices of Christian Universalism.

It is certain that Kenneth Patton understood the radical nature of the mission he had been given. He accepted as his charge the breaking of new ground and reconceiving the message and the method of liberal religion. He is quoted as saying, "Granted that our roots were in the Judeo-Christian tradition, but do we have to be stuck in the rut in which we originated?" A clearer affirmation of the vision of the New Universalism would be hard to find.

The church Patton envisioned was, indeed, a significant alternative to the tradition bound churches of Boston. Within a classic New England meeting-house structure, he created a church which was different visually—a church in the round, integrating symbols and art from the world's great religions and cultures, centered around an inlaid map of the globe and focused upon a mural of the great nebula in Andromeda—instead of an altar, a shelf of books containing scriptures from religious traditions from around the world.

Patton's Charles Street Meeting House was more than a visual challenge to conventional thinking. Its patterns of worship burst the bonds of habit and custom. One midwestern Universalist, returning from a visit to Boston in 1960, reported to her small, rural Universalist church that in the Charles Street Meeting House, on the Sunday she attended, a May pole had been erected and as part of the service, the congregation danced around it, all ages were involved, and the elements of the service were from world religions and modern poets. And, she reported, it was "real worship!" She came home with mimeographed copies of services from the Meeting House and a clear intent to adapt those materials to her church. The excitement betrayed by that report made it clear that the understanding of religion had been significantly enlarged for this woman and for her audience in rural Ohio. Inevitably, the experiment in Boston began to be replicated in small ways across the continent.

Patton himself was conscious of breaking new ground theologically and liturgically. Addressing a gathering of Universalists in Blanchester, Ohio, in 1958, Patton described himself as "a man on a bicycle." While on his journey, he said, he had come across this group of people called Universalists. He had stopped to visit with them and found they were a kind, thoughtful, gentle people. But he could not tarry long with them. He was on a journey, a religious journey, a personal journey. He would be pleased to have them accompany him, but he was not willing to forgo his journey in order to remain in their company. If the Universalists were unable to journey with him, he would wish them a fond farewell, for his future would be found on the road, not beside it.

In his Berry Street Lecture, "The Plentitude of Being" (1965), Patton sought to outline the philosophical and theological assumptions which guided him on his journey, and which he had attempted to incarnate in the Charles Street Meeting House. He called for a liberal religion which was experientially based and which was socially, economically, and politically relevant. He defined "plenitude of being" as "that state wherein there is a total focusing of the attention and powers of the person upon every act of experience; it is the state of being wholly alive, wholly engaged." He argued that "If a man [*sic*] can be moved from being centered in the self, in the family, in the town, to becoming identified with and related to the nation, the continent, and then the world, he can find in himself the width, the emotions of belonging, and the understanding to make all the world his home of being."

And later in the same lecture he said, "Whereas the traditional mystic seeks to achieve oneness with God, the naturalistic mystic seeks to know his actual and living oneness with nature and with humanity."

The poems, readings, hymns, and services which Patton created for the Charles Street Meeting House reflected this naturalistic mysticism, celebrating the human experience in its natural setting, embracing the whole of the human experience as one common legacy, and defining the planet as our common home. The liturgy Patton created for the Charles Street Meeting House sang of salvation in this world, called for justice in this world, rejoiced in the rhythm of the seasons, and celebrated life and death. The Meeting House Press, established by Patton, made the world and the experience of the experimental congregation available to the larger movement.

It is clear that the Charles Street Meeting House was designed to respond to the theological crisis of Universalism as it struggled to reverse its decline. Merger with the Unitarians interrupted that process before its full consequences could be known. But this much seems clear: The Charles Street Meeting House, embodying as it did Kenneth Patton's liturgical vision, shaped the thinking and the worshipping of Unitarians and Universalists alike, providing them a common language and common experiences which prepared the road to merger. It was in the Charles Street Meeting House, under the leadership of Kenneth Patton, that a stumble-footed humanism learned to dance and a monotone rationalism learned to sing. Because of the Charles Street Meeting House, Unitarian Universalism would never again be the same.

What may be less clear is that the Universalist experiment at the Charles Street Meeting House represented a response to a larger challenge. The Second World War had destroyed the insular and parochial world in which western civilization had evolved. In its place was an increasingly integrated, mutually interdependent global civilization in which ancient traditions and cultures suddenly found themselves confronting and challenging each other. What is more, this cultural confrontation was occurring in the context of a densely armed world that seemed never more than thirty minutes from destruction. Religion, the keeper of tradition and custom, would either offer a route to global accommodation or it would be one more source of dangerous conflict.

The Charles Street Meeting House under the leadership of Kenneth Patton represented an effort to find a religious path adequate to this strange, challenging, promising world. In many ways, the experiment at Charles Street was Universalism's bold effort to create "a religion for one world"—a religion which could find in the varied faiths human beings have embraced echoes and resonances which could enlarge and enrich conventional western traditions and understandings. This was not an attempt to create a "least common denominator world religion" but to enter into a conversation in which narrow parochialism could be refined and opened to deeper and richer insight in the context of respectful encounter with the vast history of human religious speculation. Patton understood that the diverse traditions of the human community are not interchangeable, but he acted on the faith that beneath the apparent chaos of the religious venture, there is an underlying order resulting from a common human encounter with time and death and the plentitude of being—an order which made the insights of various cultures translatable. He sought to make those insights accessible by creating a religious expression that could lift people out of their little local universes and situate them firmly in the larger context of the total human venture, the incomprehensibly vast evolutionary universe.

The Charles Street Meeting House was a bold and daring venture. It was the consequence and the outgrowth of the insights, efforts, dreams, and hopes of women and men who envisioned a New Universalism—one which would prove adequate to the times and the circumstances of a world suddenly grown small and intimate and threatened. Because of this remarkable experiment, the Universalists brought to the merger with the Unitarians in 1961 an incredible richness resulting from decades of struggling for a new identity and a greater sense of the role of liberal religion in relation to Christianity and to the new world which was becoming a global village.

Sadly, in the years since merger Unitarian Universalism has not fully embraced the richness of insight, of vision, of faith and promise that the Charles Street Meeting House incarnated. Energy and resources have been expended on perfecting institutional structures. More significantly, much of the old landscape has been revisited, trying to fit Unitarian Universalist experience into the language and categories of traditional Christian thought. The dream of a "universalized Universalism" has faded for a generation grown timid and narrow of vision. However, for those with ears to hear, it is still possible to discern the voice of Kenneth Patton calling us to embrace the plenitude of being, calling us to see the universe as our home and the entire human venture as our legacy, and reminding us that religion is a journey, not a place to settle down. If we can train our ears to hear that voice, perhaps we may yet discover the path to a religion for one world.

Kenneth L. Patton

Photo: Wayne Armstrong

Chapter 2

Kenneth L. Patton:
A Biographical Sketch

Maryell Cleary

(From the *Dictionary of Unitarian Universalist Biography*, an on-line project of the Unitarian Universalist Historical Society, edited by Peter Hughes)

Kenneth Leo Patton (1911–1994), identified as one of the major poets and a prophet of contemporary liberal religion, was a voice for a poetic, naturalistic humanism at a time when most humanists were defining a religion of reason. Minister and scholar David Bumbaugh has summed up Patton's work: "It was he who taught a monotone rationalism how to sing; it was he who taught a stumble-footed humanism how to dance; it was he who cried 'Look!' and taught our eyes to see the glory in the ordinary."

Born in Three Oaks, a small town in western Michigan, Patton lived his early years there with his mother, brother and maternal grandparents. He never knew his father. His family belonged to a strict Methodist church. He attended two church services on Sundays, morning and evening, and in between the adults allowed no secular amusements. He recalled hearing cheers and shouts from the neighboring baseball field on Sunday afternoons, wanting to join in but not allowed to go.

When he was eight or nine Patton moved with his mother and brother to a working-class suburb of Chicago. There he graduated from high school, the first in the family to do so. He went on to junior college, working at night to finance art lessons on Saturdays. Thus began his lifelong passion for the visual arts. At the age of 20 he began writing poetry. He completed his college work at Eureka College, from which he received a B.A. in 1937.

Though he would have liked a career in art, Patton chose ministry as a way to support his family and make use of his talent in writing and speaking. While serving several Disciples of Christ churches in small mid-Illinois towns, he developed a talent for beautiful extemporaneous prayer. At the same time he commuted to the University of Chicago to work on a degree in theology. There he studied with such outstanding teachers and humanists as Edward Scribner Ames, Henry Nelson Wieman and A. Eustace Haydon. Haydon, who spoke in poetic language with a beautifully modulated voice, influenced Patton greatly. He showed the younger man that religion could be much more than a set of dogmas, that it could include all the arts as well. Patton received an M.A. in 1939 and a B.D. in 1940.

In 1942 Haydon suggested that Patton, now a confirmed humanist, apply for the open pulpit of the First Unitarian Society of Madison, Wisconsin. Patton did so, was called, and served until January 1949. He helped the Society obtain the services of famed architect Frank Lloyd Wright for the design of its new building. While in Madison, he published his first three books: *Strange Seed*, 1946, a slim volume of lyric poetry; *Beyond Doubt*, 1946, a collection of radio talks; and *Hello, Man*, 1945, poetry and poetic prose which celebrated humanism and naturalism in religion. The latter established him as a major spokesperson for this still new approach to religion.

In a radio talk Patton casually said that he would like to "resign from the white race and become a colored man." To his surprise this catapulted him into notoriety. A national magazine asked him to explore the extent of racial prejudice in Chicago by attempting to integrate restaurants, hotels, country clubs and real estate. After being repeatedly turned away when he averred himself a negro or when accompanied by people of color, Patton visited an interracial housing project. "Here we found swarms of Negro and 'white' children playing together, families of all colors living side by side," he reported in "A Personal Experience of Brotherhood," in the Unitarian *Christian Register* for December 1947. "In those two days I became colored in a more profound sense than mere verbal profession can ever consummate. I have 'crossed the line' through a deeply emotional experience and I have no desire to cross back. Where I now am is where every honest man will one day have to be."

In 1949 Patton was invited to become minister of the Charles Street Meeting House, an experimental church in Boston created by Clinton Lee Scott and the Massachusetts Universalist Convention to revitalize Universalism and to reinstate a Universalist presence in Boston. Since Universalists' traditional message, that a loving God would not condemn anyone to hell, had been accepted by other denominations, Universalists needed a new focus and a wider scope. Patton's fifteen-year ministry redefined the meaning of the word "Universalism" by bringing the arts of all religions and cultures into "a religion for one world."

Patton threw himself into this venture with both mind and body. Colleague Charles Reinhardt recalls coming into the Meeting House one morning and finding him on his knees painting a mural of the Andromeda Galaxy for the proscenium. Says Reinhardt, "He looked like a happy kid building a terrific model airplane." His enthusiasm was contagious. Although the Meeting House congregation was never large, a dedicated core group supported this new realization of religious art, coming regularly to Friday evening work nights. Among others, two talented artists, brother and sister Ralph and Charlotte Edlund, designed and constructed a series of large bronze symbols illustrating a broad variety of human endeavors. Today the symbols are on display at Starr King School for the Ministry in Berkeley, California. Together, Patton and his congregation built an outstanding art collection.

While at the Meeting House, Patton wrote a prodigious amount of worship material. He also arranged as hymns and readings material from great poets like Walt Whitman, and selections from the world's scriptures. Using a mimeograph machine and a printing press in the church basement, Patton published pamphlets, books and sermons as well as weekly supplements for the looseleaf hymnals. Two volumes of *Hymns of Humanity* came from the mimeograph machine, while *Man's Hidden Search*, 1954, a classic statement of naturalistic mysticism, and Clarence Skinner's *Worship and the Well-ordered Life* rolled off the printing press. Patton's most ambitious project, *A Religion for One World*, 1964, published in conjunction with Beacon Press, gave an in-depth account of this experiment in universal religion, lavishly illustrated with photographs. When the newly-merged Unitarian Universalist Association needed a new hymnal, Patton was an obvious choice for a place on the Hymnbook Commission. Many of the hymns and readings used in the Meeting House became part of *Hymns for the Celebration of Life*, 1964. Old hymn tunes came to new life with his words, as in "We are the earth upright and proud," set to "Eine Feste Burg," and "Brief our days but long for singing," set to the melody of "Jesu, Joy of Man's Desiring."

Patton's outspoken and provocative preaching offended many, including his more conservative colleagues in the Massachusetts Universalist Convention. He jousted verbally with other ministers and religious leaders. His inability to be a pastoral minister drove parishioners away. His single-mindedness led him to ignore others' concerns and to respond with irritation to their needs. Often tendentious, he refused to compromise or even listen to other points of view. In practice, as a minister, he charged ahead with his own projects and relied on lay leadership to take care of church finances and membership growth.

Patton was twice married. In junior college he had met and married Elizabeth Pfeifer, with whom he had five children. After being divorced, he married Mitzi Anderson around 1960. They had two children.

In 1964 the Unitarian Society of Ridgewood, New Jersey invited Patton to become its minister. At this time he felt the need of a larger and more secure income and a home for his family outside the center city. For a while he served both congregations, coming to Boston once a month; then reluctantly left the Meeting House.

In Ridgewood Patton reconstituted Meeting House Press in order to publish more of his works. *The Sense of Life*, 1974, was a sensitive look at the natural world and the integral role of humanity in it. *A Religion of Realities*, 1977, summed up of Patton's religion and philosophy of life. The meditation manual *Songs of Simple Thanksgiving*, 1978, celebrated simplicity in a range of items, from the ordinary elegance of handmade tools to those seemingly complicated and mysterious phenomena, human beings and stars. All in all, Patton wrote nearly thirty books, as well as anthologizing an immense amount of humanistic-oriented poetry from around the world.

As a minister, Patton was an iconoclast. He disdained any special treatment as a clergyman. He would not call himself "Reverend," saying that he was no more to be revered than anyone else. He never used the honorific, "Doctor," though entitled to do so by an honorary degree. He refused to wear a pulpit robe, even at his own installation service. He did not preach sermons, he gave addresses, and not in a church sanctuary but in a meeting house.

Patton did not join organizations for the liberation of any group or to promote any social issue, yet he preached powerful sermons on such subjects. Controversial organizations, including the Communist Party, found space for their gatherings at the Meeting House. In his early works he used "man" as a synonym for the human race, as was usual in those times. Later, he used inclusive language; he also revised some of his earlier writings in that way. He praised unstintingly writers, such as Carl Sagan, Richard Leakey, Jane Goodall, Lewis Thomas, and Loren Eiseley, whose work he admired for insight into nature and contemporary science. He wrote of his own sense of identification with the natural process— "We love the world, loving ourselves as part of the world"—and of his feelings of wonder: "That day I see a leaf is a marvel of a day. Many days I see millions of leaves without seeing one leaf."

Patton received many honors. They included the Religious Arts Guild award in 1964, an honorary Doctor of Humane Letters from Meadville/Lombard Theological School in 1967, the Bragg Award for Distinguished Service to Humanism in 1980, and the Unitarian Universalist Association's Distinguished Service Award in 1986.

He retired in 1986 and died of congestive heart failure in his Ridgewood home on Christmas Day, 1994. He will be particularly remembered for the hymns and readings used so often in liberal religious services. Perhaps most often used, and most familiar, is the reading "Let Us Worship." Here are a few lines:

Let us worship with eyes, ears, and fingertips.
Let us love the world through heart and mind and body.
Let us worship, and let us learn to love.

Patton papers can be found in the Vincent Silliman Collection at the Meadville/Lombard Theological School Library in Chicago, Illinois; at the Starr King School for the Ministry Library in Berkeley, California; and in the Charles Street Metting House Collection at the Andover-Harvard Theological Library in Cambridge, Massachusetts. In addition to the books mentioned in the article above, Patton wrote *Man Is the Meaning* (1956), a minister's manual; *The Ground of Being* (1962), meditations and readings; *This World, My Home* (1966), poetic readings; *Services and Songs for the Celebration of Life* (1967); *The Way for This Journey* (1976), based upon the *Tao te ching; Kaggen* (1976), based upon South African Bushman folklore; *The Happy Atheist* (1984), essays; and *The Chinese Poets* (1984), based upon Chinese poetry. His books of poetry include *Recognition* (1960), *All Blessedness* (1975), *Strange Harvest* (1976), and *The Intimate Enemy* (1984). *The Visitor and Hello, Man* (1947) contains poetry and autobiographical material as well as a reprint of *Hello, Man. The Wonder of Life* (1997), edited by Maryell Cleary, is an anthology of Patton's work. Biographical information on Patton can be obtained in Wayne Armstrong's obituary, "Kenneth Leo Patton," in the *UUA Directory, 1995–96,* and in Doris Armstrong, *Unitarians in Ridgewood* (1997).

Chapter 3

The Poetic Prophet

James D. Hunt

The following four selections are from the works of Kenneth L. Patton.

The year of my birth in 1911 is emblematic, just as the movement of religious humanism was emerging in the ministries of John Dietrich and Curtis Reese. My lifetime covers the historical process of this movement. Born in the bowels of Protestant fundamentalism, I was totally unaware of it. It took me thirty years to struggle to self-knowledge. My doubts began at fifteen, and it took another fifteen years until the process culminated at the University, of Chicago, under Edward Scribner Ames, Henry Nelson Wieman, and A. Eustace Haydon.

After serving three churches in the Disciples of Christ, I became the humanist minister of the Unitarian Society of Madison, Wisconsin, in which ministry George Burman Foster, A. Eustace Haydon, James Hart, and Rupert Holloway had preceded me. Max C. Otto of the University of Wisconsin was a member of the society, and I took all the courses he offered. (1)

***

"Hello, Man"

I found myself under a friendless sky,
walking on the careless earth,
and I said to the sky,
"Hello,"
but my voice was swallowed up in the echoless vast.

I said to the earth,
"Hello,"
but the earth gave back to me only my own voice, faint
     and useless.

I thought, "Where can I say hello?
Who will give me a reply?"
The answer was clear, so I said,
"Hello, Man." (2)

***

When I arrived in humanistic Unitarianism, I had no knowledge of what the literary and devotional resources of religious naturalism might be. *Hymns of the Spirit* had recently been published, the first hymn book to contain humanistic materials. It contained some eighty nontheistic hymns and readings, some of questionable literary merit. Inured to the wealth and majesty of the literature of the Old Testament and the parables of the New Testament, and a two-thousand-year accumulation of Christian hymns and writings, this was a watery gruel indeed.

I was saddled with a mission. I must find content for the naturalistic pronouncement and celebration. I have spent thirty-six years in the search, and much is still undiscovered.

I had begun writing poetry when I was twenty, and had filled several notebooks, but nothing had been published. . . . Because of the redolence of clichés in hymnody, it took several years before I found courage to attempt a hymn verse. My writings accumulated. One summer I was asked to lead the evening services at the Lake Geneva Summer Assembly. I wrote a series of longer pieces for that occasion. Some people from Omaha, Nebraska, who ran a press, asked if I would like them to print a book for me. This led to three ventures in publishing, the third in collaboration with Beacon Press in Boston.

The first book was *Hello, Man,* published in 1945 when I was thirty-four, after I had been writing for fourteen years. Happily none of my juvenilia has been printed, and never will be. (3)

***

"The Man Jesus"

Jesus, you were the man of my vision and dreaming; you were the perfect creature without stain or blemish;
    the never sinning, the unmistaken, the all-loving
    the all-knowing;
you were the end of creation; the fullest and completest point in history and time;
you were the goal, the apex, the unattainable being
    very God himself.

Jesus, you were the beacon light to my spirit, the anchor of
    my hope, the searchlight in the darkness leading
    me;

you were my hero, my guide, my teacher, the not-
to-be-questioned, the gladly accepted, savior,
redeemer, friend.

Unto you, Jesus, did I cling even when I rejected your
father, God himself.

You were still perfect man when perfect god was gone.

You were the last rock to which I clung in the sea of flux
and change.

You were the last to walk the tossing waters and not to
sink therein.

Yet there was that within me which would not permit you,
Jesus, to walk alone, the perfect one in a world of
imperfection.

There was that within me which could not hold forever
onto you, that forced me to shove off from you to
swim by myself in the sea.

For there grew within me the knowledge that you too were
but a swimmer in the sea, and that the sea at last
closed over you, as it will one day close over me.

I have lost you, Jesus my idol, the unscaleable
mountain, my God.

But I have found you again, Jesus my friend, my companion, my brother, who once dreamed even as now I
dream, who lost as I shall lose, who died as I shall
die. (4)

Reflections by James Hunt

In 1947, the year before I entered college at Tufts, the Universalists of Massachusetts decided to establish a new church in downtown Boston where there had been no Universalist church for years. They bought a fine old building at the foot of Beacon Hill and established it as the Charles Street Universalist Meeting House. In 1948, Ken was chosen to lead the experiment and remained 16 years until 1964.

My relation to Ken was profound, although I was just an intermittent visitor in my college years and after. Here are my memoirs:

The first church I joined was Ken's church. I liked the name "meeting house," which was very old New England, and I liked it because it didn't say "church." I was attracted to Ken because he wasn't going to try to make me believe in God.

Ken was an artist and a poet, and the more liberal he became, the less he was satisfied with the ways of Unitarian and Universalist worship, which were usually watered-down Protestant services with the Trinity left out. He was determined to use his new church as a laboratory for experiments in worship, and in this he was immensely successful, for he spearheaded a reform in Universalist and Unitarian religious practice. I was there to watch this process as he began in that big old meeting house with his tiny congregation.

He began to create fresh worship materials to replace the old prayers and Bible readings. Some of those were gathered from all the religions of the world, and some from the poets and philosophers. Some he wrote himself. He created what he called "the open hymnal," a spring-bound notebook in which could be inserted fresh hymns and readings for each week, vastly expanding the range of available materials.

At the head of the church, in place of an altar, he installed an enormous bookcase, which was to contain all the bibles of the world, all the poets and philosophers, or at least a good sampling of them. He made a point of going to the bookcase during the service and selecting the appropriate readings. Then he put in a big hi-fi system, which he operated from the pulpit. This was very unusual in 1950. It made it possible to bring in all the music of all the cultures of the world. Finally, he began a symbol project. He and some members made brass symbols of the religions and of human concerns—crosses of many kinds, crescents, stars, the sun, Yin and Yang, the lotus, peace, the atom, the wheel, the United Nations, and so forth.

The greatest symbol of all was a 29-foot painting of our neighbor in space, the spiral nebula in Andromeda. This star cluster, much like our own sun's Milky Way, was done in fluorescent paint, which in the evening was lit by black light.

The readings and the sermons were the main thing in the service. Both tended to be rather long. After the service there would be coffee and discussion, which were not common among liberal churches in those days either.

Another selection by Kenneth L. Patton

"Devotional"

If death is with me in every breath I draw, if the grave is an endless ditch beside which I must walk, and its edge may crumble and let me in any moment, still I must walk carelessly and breathe the air with a grand extravagance.

Stranger, I may never see you again, the sun upon your shoulders and our brotherliness untried, but I will drink you in as we pass as if you were an old comrade whom I now see after many years of absence, and will never see again.

Golden sky, tomorrow you may be shut from me by the earth, and the light may be gone forever from me, but I will hail you as if I were to endure as infinitely as the outreaches of your space, and this moment I will denizen eternity, fragile and temporary creature that I am.

I shall plan to read all the books in the world.

I shall love as if I possessed the time and spirit to be the companion of every man on earth.

I shall dream as if the eternities were mine to work that the dream might be fulfilled.

I will open my hand to the poor as if mine were the riches to satisfy all the needs of my fellows.

I shall set my table to feed all my hungry brothers.

I will stand against the tragedy of the world as if my confidence could encourage all the timid, as if my joy could bring delight to every stricken man, as if I could change every failure to triumph, as if I could make life to spring up as flowers wherever death has placed his feet.

And I shall also be the opposite of this.

I shall bow to tragedy as if my weeping could quell the grief of all who weep, as if my melancholy could bring sleep to all the sleepless, as if my mourning could release the bereaved from the shroud of their loss.

If then I do no more than any man can do, this at least can be said, that I closed the door to no man who would have entered, that I denied no man friendship who would have been my friend, that I did not fail to comfort any whom I held power to comfort, that I denied laughter to no one who would have laughed with me.

I shall have been an open and wall-less room where any man could have entered if he would.

> I shall go to sleep that last time, eager to awaken to another day, even if that sleep is forever and all tomorrows shall be closed to me. (5)

Reflections by James Hunt

The Meeting House was always interesting in another way. It was continually a center of controversy, and not only because a humanist was a rare bird among the New England Unitarians and Universalists. Ken believed in the prophetic function of the church and used the pulpit to freely criticize the Universalists and Unitarians and the arms race and the Cold War. One time he was approached to allow the use of his church for a fundraiser for the Communist party newspaper, *The Daily Worker,* which was losing its readers in the McCarthy era. Ken believed in the freedom of the press, and he let them hold their concert.

One day soon afterwards I visited the Meeting House and found Ken in work clothes, swabbing up oil and grease from his own printing press in the basement. He had been warned that the Boston Fire Department was about to make a fire inspection, the purpose being to close down the church in retaliation for his radicalism.

In many ways Patton's church was more like a museum than a congregation. It was full of interesting objects. He had started an art collection. Ken impressed me with his creativity, and he gave me the idea that a minister could be much like an artist, creating images and meanings. He reinforced the idea that liberal religion is something that we construct.

The Universalists in those days had a statement of faith that was repeated in many churches. It had one line that I especially liked. It said that we believed "in the authority of truth, known or to be known." That's what attracted me. I was so surprised to find a church that wasn't claiming to have all the answers.

Ken Patton's humanism showed me a way of making a constructive theology, or philosophy of life. I read his poetry and heard his sermons and I responded to his mystical view of the human community as something that is our heritage at the same time that it is something that we have to work to make real.

Ken's innovations were creative: the open hymnal (assembled each week), the discussion period, the bookcase, the sound system, the mural of the great nebula in Andromeda (symbol of the universe), the shape of the assembly (circular pews), the symbol project (65 symbols), the art collection from many cultures, prints of Kaethe Kollwitz (daughter of a leader of the Free Congregation movement in Germany, 1867–1945), the Meeting House Press (pamphlets, sermons, books for worship, other books, etc.), developing a temple for universal religion.

Ken was a tiger for research—world religions, cultures, music, art, and especially poetry. He read Walt Whitman and declared him our first great poetic prophet. Ken spent a whole summer exhaustively searching through *Leaves of Grass*. Later, on a six-month sabbatical, he spent his whole time in the poetry stacks of the Library of Congress "going over a million volumes of poetry." He then declared our second great poetic prophet to be Pablo Neruda.

Ken went to the Ridgewood, NJ, UU church in 1964, and stayed until 1986. He was a member of the Hymnbook commission for the 1964 *Hymns for the Celebration of Life*.

Another selection by Kenneth L. Patton

"Let Us Worship"

Let us worship with our eyes and ears
and fingertips; let us love the world
through heart and mind and body.

> The rushing of the wind and the pouring
> of the sun gather us together with blessing
> and comfort.

The colors flowing in the field and sky,
light over eyes, over faces, the windy colors
and the colors of warm, tideless gardens, heal our
spirits and feed our hungers.

The lifting sounds of trees and grasses,
the noises of men and women eddy into
songs of human togetherness.

The purity of birds singing, the music of throat and
brass and wood, these are golden to the ear lonely for
beauty.

We feed our eyes upon the mystery and
revelation in the faces of our brothers and
sisters.

We seek to know the wistfulness of the very young
and the very old, the wistfulness of men and women in
all times of life.

We seek to understand the
shyness behind arrogance, the
fear behind pride, the tenderness
behind clumsy strength
the anguish behind cruelty.

We live a thousand lives as we
walk through the city.

All life flows into a great common life,
if we will only open our eyes to our companions.

We listen to the secret voices of poetry and
know that all people share our yearning.

All are lonely as we are lonely, and all
need the sure presence of those who love and
are loved.

Let us worship, not in bowing down,
not with closed eyes and stopped ears.

Let us worship with the opening of all the
windows of our beings, with the full outstretch
ing of our spirits.

Life comes with singing and laughing, with tears and
confiding, with a rising wave too great to be held in
the mind and head and body, to those who have fallen in
love with life.

Let us worship, and let us learn to love. (6)

***

"P. S."

I am what I am when I am it.
I am what I am, God damn it. (7)

Notes

1. From one of Ken's catalogs from Ridgewood, New Jersey. In it there is a "Historical Postscript" taken from his book *A Religion of Realities*, Meeting House Press, Ridgewood, NJ 1977.
2. This poem, "Hello, Man," seems to be autobiographical: *The Visitor and Hello Man*, The Beacon Press, Boston, 1947: p. 127.
3. From one of Ken's catalogs from Ridgewood, New Jersey. In it there is a "Historical Postscript" taken from his book *A Religion of Realities*.
4. *V&HM*, p. 163.
5. *V&HM*, p. 54.
6. *Hello, Man*, p. 187.
7. *Strange Seed*, p. 30.

Chapter 4

He Lives Tomorrow:
Clinton Lee Scott, Revitalizer of Universalism

Charles A. Howe

When Clinton Lee Scott died on September 28, 1985, his ninety-eighth birthday, he was the oldest Unitarian Universalist minister both in age and length of service, and widely respected and loved.(1) In 1964 Beacon Press had published his book, *These Live Tomorrow: Twenty Unitarian Universalist Biographies* (reprinted 1987).(2) If there is ever another reprinting, it would be appropriate to include as an afterword yet another short biography, one of Scott himself, for he, too, through his many contributions to the ongoing life of the Unitarian Universalist movement, "lives tomorrow."

Scott's contributions have not been sufficiently appreciated by historians.(3) Thus one of the purposes of this article is to help establish Scott as a figure of importance in the history of Unitarian Universalism. He was, however, widely appreciated by those who knew him, as well as by the denomination, which in 1977 presented him with its Award for Distinguished Service in the Cause of Liberal Religion.

Clinton Lee Scott was born on a farm in Newport, Vermont, in 1887. As a youth he worked as a granite and marble cutter. His ambition, however, was to be a lawyer, and so to prepare himself for law school he entered Goddard Seminary in Barre. There a toss of a coin sent him off in a new direction. He and his roommate had accepted jobs to pump the organs in two local churches, and they tossed a coin to determine who would go where. Young Scott ended up at the Universalist church and was so inspired by the approach to religion he found there that he entered Tufts College to prepare for the Universalist ministry. After receiving his bachelor of arts degree from Tufts in 1914 and his bachelor of sacred theology degree from its Crane Theological School the following year, he was ordained at the church in Northfield, Vermont. For the next thirty-one years he served without interruption in the parish ministry.(4)

Scott was both a religious liberal—he became a humanist early in his career—and a political liberal, a socialist throughout his whole adult life. His views often caused controversy. At Buffalo, in his second parish, he narrowly escaped losing his ministerial fellowship for his pacifist views during the First World War.(5) In Atlanta, he was attacked by the local Methodist bishop as a dangerous heretic.(6) While in Peoria, he signed the *Humanist Manifesto* and crusaded against the gambling syndicate, a crusade that caused his whole family to be harassed and threatened.(7)

In 1942, in response to the urgent request of Robert Cummins, general superintendent of the Universalist denomination, he accepted a call to the Independent Christian Church in Gloucester, Massachusetts, the "mother church" of American Universalism that had been founded in 1779 by John Murray. That church was then in desperate need of new leadership.(8) It was while he was there that Scott wrote most of his witty *Parish Parables* with their keen insight into human nature and the ways of congregations.(9)

In the fourth year of his ministry in Gloucester the superintendency of the Massachusetts Universalist Convention became vacant. The churches in the Convention were having a difficult time, many of them being in a state of decline both in membership and morale, their message of Christian Universalism becoming steadily less relevant. Clarence Skinner, dean of the Crane Theological School at Tufts, urged that Scott, whom he knew to be a liberal with energy and new ideas, be appointed to fill the vacancy. Many of the younger members in the state also supported his appointment. Finally, after much political maneuvering, Scott, on a split vote, was elected to the position. He was hesitant to accept, never having aspired to denominational leadership and seeing himself as a parish minister, but in the end he was persuaded by his supporters.(10) Had he refused, his most significant contributions to Unitarian Universalism would have been lost, for it was during his tenure as superintendent that those contributions were made. It is on the years of his superintendency that this article will focus.

Scott, in his puckish way, wrote a parable poking fun at his qualifications for the position and his regrets about leaving Gloucester:

> Now there came to the Master of the Temple men of affairs which spake to him, saying, Come thou and be to us one that goeth abroad among the people, giving counsel to them that are in need, and an Elder among us for we have searched diligently for such a one and have found him not; verily thou, even thou, art of more value than no Elder at all. And the Master of the Temple answered and said, How hardly shall I be one that giveth counsel seeing I have not wisdom sufficient to mine own use? Then did the men of affairs give answer saying, Verily we know that thou art not wise, but they that have wisdom consent not to be our Elder. But thou hast a bald pate and a beard; moreover thou hast a solemn countenance, and these seemeth to the multitude a sign of wisdom. And if thou openeth not thy mouth too frequently thy lack of wisdom will not be revealed unto men.
>
> And with divers such arguments was the Master of the Temple persuaded to leave the Great Congregation and go about among the people, even an Elder in Israel. And there was a great heaviness upon him when he remembered them of the Great Congregation, yet remembered he also Lot's wife and dared not turn back. (11)

And not looking back, he plunged into his new work. Skinner imme-diately sent off a letter of congratulations:

> Dear Scott,
>
> I heard by the underground route that you have been elected superintendant [*sic*]. Congratulations to the Church and to you! So far as I know I was the first one to boom you for the position, so I feel a great deal of satisfaction in seeing you ascend the throne.
>
> Our church desperately needs real liberal leadership and I am confident that you will be able to give it. [U]se me in any way you see fit. Best wishes for a long and happy reign.
>
> Cordially,
> C. R. SKINNER(12)

Scott went to work in earnest—visiting churches, placing ministers, participating in services of ordination and installation, arranging radio addresses, writing, speaking, preaching, counseling, and generally pro-moting and strengthening the Universalist cause in Massachusetts in any way he could.

The Convention had shortly before adopted a plan of growth known as "10-10" whereby each church was challenged to grow by ten percent a year for ten years in all its activities, thus doubling its membership and strengthening its programs.(13) On assuming the superintendency, Scott immediately began to promote the plan, urging the ministers to get behind it and give it their full support.(14) Then, as a means of unifying the Convention and promoting its programs, Scott, with the Board's approval, initiated publication of a small periodical, the *Bay State Universalist*, with five issues a year. The first issue appeared in September 1946 with the follow-ing rationale for its existence, written by Scott as editor:

> Here is Volume 1-No. 1 of the *Bay State Universalist*, con-ceived and born out of the sheer necessity of propagating the faith. The task of our individual Universalist churches

in Massachusetts is so urgent and so important that it requires the concerted effort of us all, the sharing of one another in plans, techniques and encouragement.

We need to communicate with those whose aims, problems and successes are like our own, to benefit by their experience and to be warned by their mistakes.

We want every Universalist in Massachusetts to receive and read the *BSU*. The contents will be brief always, interesting sometimes, and irritating occasionally. (15)

For some of the more conservative Christian Universalists, the *Bay State Universalist* was undoubtedly not just occasionally irritating, but always irritating, since it forthrightly promoted new, more inclusive views of Universalism. The Humiliati, a small group of Crane students and alumni who had dedicated themselves to the renewal of the denomination, had promoted as a symbol of Universalism a circle with an off-center cross. The circle represented the inclusive nature of Universalism, and the off-center cross, while recognizing Universalism's Christian origin, at the same time signified that Christianity was no longer necessarily central.(16) The "10-10 Committee" had adopted this symbol to promote its work,(17) and Scott proceeded to display it prominently on the new periodical's cover page. The cover page also regularly featured short expositions of a modern, inclusive Universalism written by liberals like Skinner, Cummins, Harold Scott (the editor's brother), and Earle McKinney, David Cole, Gordon McKeeman and Albert Ziegler of the Humiliati. The first issue, for example, began with an interpretation of Universalism by Ziegler which declared that "Universalist beliefs are not based on tradition but on the demands of life today" and that the "great affirmations of Universalism do not deal with the time-worn word-pictures so long associated with religion, God, Christ, Holy Scripture, Heaven, Salvation, and so forth. Its message on these truths of another age is negative, as it must be on all conceptions which lag behind the experience of man."(18)

Scott was convinced that Universalism must undergo some basic changes if it was to survive, and he was committed to helping make these changes take place. The overall tone of the magazine was not polemical, however. "Can we help?" he asked in that first issue. "Where is your trouble? Religious Education? Finance? Membership? Attendance? Organization? Program? Can we help by Mail? Can we help by Counsel? Can we help by a Visit?"(19)

A regular feature of the *Bay State Universalist* was a column by Scott called "Third Floor Back," referring to the location of his office at denominational headquarters at 16 Beacon Street in Boston. In it he included a miscellany of short items about anything he felt his readers should know, including the fact that the door to "Third Floor Back" was always open to those who needed his help "from nine or earlier, to five or later" except for Saturdays, Sundays and holidays.(20) Another occasional feature was "Pilgrim Parables," a continuation of the "Parish Parables" written in Gloucester, albeit in a new context.(21)

One way in which Scott broadened the Convention's communications network and retained and added members was through the establishment in 1947 of the Larger Fellowship of Universalists, patterned after the Unitarian Church of the Larger Fellowship, which had been organized several years earlier. Scott had been enthusiastic about the Unitarian project and was quick to organize a Universalist counterpart upon assuming the superintendency.(22)

Yet another way in which Scott went about promoting Universalism was through weekly radio broadcasts which he initiated in the fall of 1946 as part of the "10-10" program. The original series, "Universalism Speaks," consisted of Monday evening talks presented by a variety of ministers,(23) but a year later the format was changed, with Scott himself delivering Sunday morning addresses under the title "Religion Can Make Sense. "(24) This was a demanding task, not only because of the weekly schedule, but also because a full manuscript was required and he was accustomed to speaking from only minimal notes. The writing of these addresses was to bear long-term fruits, however, for their texts were to provide the material for a popular, standard book on liberal religion, also titled *Religion Can Make Sense*, which has gone through numerous printings.(25) In January 1949 Scott turned the broadcasts over to Kenneth L. Patton, minister of the newly established Charles Street Meeting House, a move that was later to result in serious controversy.(26)

In 1947 the Universalist Church of America held its biennial General Assembly at St. Lawrence University in Canton, New York. It proved to be a stormy meeting and marked a turning point for the denomination, for it was here that the "young Turks," many of them from Massachusetts, first showed their strength. One result was the election of Mary Slaughter Scott, Clinton's wife, to the U.C.A. Board of Trustees. This was accomplished by "bullet balloting" promoted by the young liberal ministers, a strategy whereby many delegates were persuaded to vote only for Mary, even though they were entitled to vote for several candidates for the Board. It was a ploy that infuriated some of the conservatives. (27) Mary Slaughter Scott was a fourth-generation Universalist from Camp Hill, Alabama—a strong-minded "peppery" woman with progressive views who was serving as a denominational field worker in religious education when she and Clinton met.(28) Following their marriage in 1930 — it was Clinton's second; he was a widower with two daughters— Mary remained heavily involved in church affairs, working closely with her husband.(29) Her election to the U.C.A. Board was seen as a major coup by the liberals.

At this same biennial Frederick May Eliot, President of the American Unitarian Association, proposed that Universalists and Unitarians again consider denominational merger. The Federal Council of Churches had for the second time rejected the Universalist application for membership on theological grounds, so it seemed a propitious time for Eliot to make this overture.(30) Scott had always opposed Universalist membership in the F.C.C. and responded positively to the idea of merger, as did many of the liberals in the denomination, including the Humiliati and other young ministers from Massachusetts.(31) Many of the conservatives, on the other hand, felt threatened by Eliot's suggestion, fearing that Universalism's traditional Christian emphasis would be lost in such a merger. An ideological split in the denomination was beginning to become apparent. In Massachusetts, the State Convention became the focal point for this division. On one side were the proponents of traditional Christian Universalism; on the other, the proponents of the new, emergent Universalism. While Clinton Scott's sympathies were certainly with the latter, he tried hard to administer his office impartially.

A controversy developed over the off-center cross symbol on the cover of the *Bay State Universalist*, the traditionalists seeing it as a move away from the historical Universalist position. At last, amid a mixture of applause and protest, the Convention Board voted to remove the symbol "in the interest of harmony." It is clear from his editorial comment that Scott disapproved of the move:

> Regardless of the individual interpretations which those who like the symbol and those who do not like the symbol may put on it, a distinctive emblem of Universalism is a valuable instrument of denominational publicity. No symbol adopted by the Convention would be the first choice of all our constituency, but the wide acceptance of the one we have indicates that for those whose concept of Universalism has gone beyond its historical meaning, it has proven to be quite satisfactory. (32)

Clearly the most trying experience of Clinton Scott's superintendency was the controversy surrounding the Charles Street Meeting House and its minister, Kenneth L. Patton. The 1947 annual meeting of the Massachusetts Universalist Convention had, on Scott's urging, voted to establish a church in Boston where there had been no Universalist church for a number of years despite the fact that it was the site of denominational headquarters. The new church was to be pioneering in nature, one that would offer a clear alternative to the city's Unitarian churches, which at that time were traditional and conservative.

An historic church building located at the corner of Charles and Mount Vernon streets was purchased, the Convention's office relocated there, and Scott instructed to recommend a minister. His choice was Patton, then serving as minister of the First Unitarian Society of Madison, Wisconsin, a man known for his preaching and writing skills and his openness to innovation. The Convention's Board of Trustees unanimously accepted Scott's recommendation, and Patton was installed as minister of the Charles Street Meeting House on February 2, 1949, in an impressive service attended by Universalists from all over the state.(33)

Almost at once, however, opposition arose to Patton's ministry. Scott had turned over responsibility for the Convention's weekly radio broadcasts to Patton, an outspoken naturalist humanist, and the more conservative, Christian-oriented Universalists in the area were disturbed by what they heard. They were also disturbed by the content of some of the Meeting House's newspaper advertisements. By April, prior to the Convention's annual meeting, a letter was circulated to all Universalist churches in the state expressing the concerns of six clergymen: William Wallace Rose of Lynn, Frank B. Chatterton of Cambridge, Arthur W. Webster of Salem, Leslie C. Nichols of Melrose, John E. Wood of Attleboro, and Charles H. Monbleau of Malden.(34) Four questions were raised: first, whether the Charles Street Meeting House, identified as a stronghold of humanism, was indeed a Universalist church; second, whether the Convention should provide financial support to the Meeting House indefinitely; third, whether Patton's radio broadcasts were representative of Universalism and brought credit to the Universalist name; and fourth, whether a trend toward humanism would help the Universalist cause. The signers urged that these issues be raised in the churches prior to the annual meeting and concluded by expressing their belief that the future of Universalism in Massachusetts depended on how these questions were answered.

Despite such misgivings, Convention support of the Meeting House continued. Nevertheless, opposition to Patton's ministry mounted. Many found him abrasive, tactless, and uncompromising, and projecting an image of Universalism they found unacceptable. Some churches began to reduce their financial support of the Convention; the radio station refused to broadcast Patton's Easter sermon as being too controversial; there was adverse publicity over some of the programs held at the Meeting House; attendance at Sunday services declined; some members submitted their resignations. Mary Scott, who, like Clinton, had put a great deal of time and energy into establishing the Meeting House, was disturbed by the trend of events and worked to change their course. She wrote a woman who had resigned after Patton received considerable publicity for refusing to pay his taxes in protest of government policies, urging her to reconsider:

I realize just how you feel about "cheap publicity" and the abhorrence of anything like that for our church. I haven't seen the issue of the Boston American to which you referred, but from past experience with that yellow sheet know that it can be rather bad. I think I can understand your feeling wanting to have no part in it for I feel the same way. But I'd like to present another side:

Our Universalist cause needs a church in the city of Boston. . . . And Boston—with its Catholic population increasing in numbers and political activity, with its Tremont Temple and Park Street evangelism, and with its very conservative Unitarian churches, heavily endowed and not too concerned about social issues—needs desperately the stimulus of a liberal church which is concerned about the welfare of human beings.

It has been Clinton Scott's dream that . . . a church might be built in Boston, a Universalist Church which would be truly universalistic in spirit and in outlook. Few people know how much time and effort he has devoted to it . . . It hasn't been easy. . . .

Just now things look rather dark. If only we could get people to see and believe that the building of a Universalist Church is our great task, and that the creation of real universalists is a lifetime adventure. And that this task has not changed within the week's time. We do not have to agree with the minister in his recent statements [on pacifism and refusing to pay taxes]—we may even admit his right to do as he has—while we . . . feel that from the standpoint of public relations for the Church his action was a mistake. . . . Our support of the Charles Street Meeting House and being part of it need not mean that we agree with Kenneth's actions—certainly I do not agree with many of the things he says even tho I would insist on a free pulpit. . . . The church, our church, is more important than any minister or any publicity about him or it. Let's not kill the church. We want a Universalist Church in Boston long after you and I and the present minister are gone. I think we can work to build the kind of a church we want.

I hope you will reconsider your decision about resigning. We need you.(35)

Despite this eloquent appeal, the resignation was not withdrawn.(36)

A few days earlier, on a Sunday after returning from church, Mary had vented her own frustration and anger over what was happening at the Meeting House in a letter to Patton:

Dear Kenneth:

There are several things I've been wanting to say—for a long time—and I think I shall relieve my mind of them instead of inwardly sputtering. Some of us before we knew you—had a dream of building a liberal church in Boston—a Universalist Church which would be truly universalistic. Clinton Scott wanted that more than anything else—so much that he staked the success of his professional work on trying to achieve it.

Then after detailing the financial support the Convention had given Patton for his work, including publicity, she continued:

I'm awfully tired of hearing you make public aspersions of the MUC and its inability to support the church and your program. This morning in the forum period, in commenting on your recent publicity [in the media], you stated that the Mass. Convention was unable to pay anything for publicity for you, unable to give you a radio program, etc., and this [stand of yours] got you on the radio, etc., etc.

Perhaps someone should remind you that the Massachusetts Convention had a good radio program when you arrived—that it was turned over to you and that perhaps if you hadn't made that crude facetious comment about Jesus and the beer bottles—which offended our own people as well as arousing the opposition of others, we'd probably still have a radio program. . . . Probably you know that the MUC has already spent $1500 of its capital funds in the radio suit and is prepared to spend more—to defend your right to free speech. Even when a great many Universalists do not agree with you! So—it seems to me it is decidedly poor taste to keep talking about the niggardliness of the MUC.(37)

As far as your tax defiance program is concerned that, of course, is your privilege. From the standpoint of public relations and the welfare of our struggling church some people would question its wisdom. You may not be concerned about whom you offend—but Clinton Scott has to be concerned to secure the wherewithal to pay your salary. And, frankly, it burns me up that he has to spend so much of his energy explaining you and making it possible for you to "express yourself" . . . .

Just now our radio suit is up for decision. Did you consider that your tax action might influence adversely that issue? . . . Did you think what an increased "selling" problem you threw in the lap of the State Superintendent, who is so deeply concerned over the church? In the eyes of the conservatives it is bad enough to support a minister who is theologically different, to say nothing of a "treasonable" one. For some it may be the last straw.

. . . Few ministers are handed a building, a subsidized budget and an opportunity such as yours. Some of us would be glad if you'd forget the promotion of your personal program. . . . It looks as if you are entirely agreeable to crippling the work of the church in order to express yourself. Some of us would like to see you forget Kenneth

Patton for a little and work to build a universalist church in the city of Boston.

> Loyally yours,
> Mary S. Scott (38)

Clinton Scott, of course, found himself right in the middle of the controversy. He had done more than any other person to establish the Meeting House and had recommended that Patton be its minister; at the same time, he was responsible to and for all the churches in the state. It was a difficult situation, one that would have defeated a lesser man, but his good judgment, fairness, and personal integrity enabled him not only to survive, but also to retain the respect and confidence of the vast majority, even though the emotional cost must have been enormous. One can only speculate as to the nature of his conversations with Mary on the subject, and with Patton!

At the Convention's 1950 annual meeting held in Malden, controversy over the Meeting House erupted, prompting this commentary in the denomination's periodical, the *Christian Leader:*

> If there is any possible way of dispensing with state and national conventions . . . we might find that this would help us immeasurably. . . . Take Massachusetts, for instance. They had themselves a convention in May. Now, it is no secret that for some years, Massachusetts has been suffering from growing pains. But it was hoped that time would bring relief, especially after a mild, profitable 1949 meeting. Not so. 1950 dawned red-eyed and angry. No black eyes resulted, it is true, but the convention throughout was entirely too belligerent for a church meeting. It was apparent that "sides" had been chosen up beforehand, and everyone was ready to go out and win for his team. The meetings seethed with people passing on to other "safe" people the party strategy. There was little, if any, respect for the "opposition" (who, incidentally, were

fellow Universalists!). In the course of the struggle, personalities were indulged in, anger was shown, characters were defamed, and there was even deliberate evasion of the rules . . . [S]ome strange things did happen, as when a budget was voted granting eight thousand dollars aid in the coming year to the Boston church, while, in a later vote, the same church was denied fellowship in the State Convention. Thousands for charity, but not even a hand in fellowship!(39)

Then at the 1951 annual meeting, held in Haverhill, in a highly charged atmosphere, a motion to discontinue funding of the Meeting House was narrowly defeated on a roll call vote.(40) Just prior to that meeting, Gilbert Potter, minister of the church at Fitchburg and chairman of the Convention's committee on recommendations, had sent a letter to all churches setting a deadline for the receipt of recommendations. He then added the following:

One of the most serious issues facing the Convention this year is the problem of the Charles Street Universalist Meeting House. That you may be familiar with a sample of the type of preaching emanating from its pulpit under the present leadership, I am enclosing a copy of a sermon for your reading. The President of the Convention, Mr. Chester A. Dunlap, will be interested to receive your reactions with respect to this preachment.(41)

Enclosed was a copy of a sermon by Patton titled "The Prostitution of the Clergy," its thesis being that most ministers, in order to retain their positions, sacrificed their integrity in order to please those who paid their salaries.

Reactions to Potter's letter were swift and strong. Patton himself sent a letter to all Convention churches, not, as he put it, "as a defense of myself, . . . [for] I do not consider that I have done or said anything for which I need to defend myself," but rather to raise questions regarding ministerial ethics, copyright laws, freedom of the pulpit, the autonomy of the local congregation, and the freedom of a financially-aided church.(42) Scott also responded quickly, writing Dunlap that he considered Potter's action to be clearly unethical, and expressing his reluctance "to believe that the Massachusetts Universalist Convention or its officials would be party to any such procedure. "(43) He also wrote leaders of both the Universalist and Unitarian denominational ministers' associations, expressing the need for a code of ethical conduct for Universalist ministers.(44)

Other ministers joined in condemning Potter's action, among them Charles Reinhardt at Saugus, Heber Robinson at Beverly and Essex, Francis Rockwell at Cambridge, and Ray Sabin at Peabody, all of whom also condemned John Wood for unethical conduct in calling for Patton's resignation;(45) Carl Westman at Gloucester;(46) Ronald Kister at Swampscott;(47) and David Hicks MacPherson, student minister at Foxborough.(48) While there were probably those who supported Potter, they for the most part found it politic to remain silent, or at least not to put their sentiments in writing. Some ministers urged the state ministers' association to take action condemning Potter, but apparently this was never done.(49)

All in all, by forcefully raising the issues of congregational autonomy and freedom of the pulpit, the incident appears to have blunted the force of the attacks on Patton and the Meeting House. The attacks were not quite over, however. The Melrose church, in March 1953, petitioned the Convention to either change the type of program conducted at the Meeting House or to cut off all financial support.(50) Through all this, Scott stood firm in his support of Patton. When the Malden church, as a protest, paid only four dollars of its Convention quota, Scott replied as follows:

> I feel it to be within my duty to defend Charles Street
> Church against your statement that its program "degrades
> Universalism," even as it is my habit to defend any one of
> our churches against any such unfair charge. Furthermore
> I resent your remark because Charles Street is my church
> and its minister is my minister. I and the six members of
> my immediate family hold membership in this church. We

who are members of the Charles Street Church like it and know it is doing good work. It is a principle practiced in all denominations with congregational government, and even those of Episcopal polity, that the program of the church is determined by its congregation. This principle should be as inviolable among Universalists as it is among Congregationalists and Episcopalians.(51)

Not unexpectedly, the attacks took their toll on Patton, as is evident from a letter written to Scott following a particularly difficult Convention Board meeting at which he had lost his temper:

> I've gone through hell the last three years. That a basically introspective, introverted, thin-skinned person like myself could have gotten involved in such a [situation] demonstrates my ignorance and fool-hardiness. I have been on the verge of a nervous smash-up several times. My personal life and my family life have also been partial casualties.
>
> But I'm a stubborn bastard, if nothing else. I'll make this thing go, or I'll die trying. If it can't work out with one system, we'll invent another. Frankly, the sentimental, middle-class, tender-minded, conservative, thick-headed people in the Universalist denomination do not bother me essentially. The world is full of their kind. I have known for a long time that what I have to do will be done in spite of them. I take some ironic satisfaction that as much of their precious money as has already been spent has gone to buy something like our project. And when billions are being spent on the trash of war, materialism and poobah, don't expect me to feel guilty that we have rescued a few thousand for creative and prophetic religion.
>
> Ambivalent as I am, and with all the hell it has cost me, I am still glad I came to Boston, and I would probably have come if I had known everything beforehand that

> I learned after arrival. I consider you my friend, and I bear
> you no resentment personally. Sometimes I am amazed at
> your patience, and I am constantly heartened by your out-
> spoken integrity.(52)

Thirty-five years later, after Scott's death, Patton expressed his indebted-
ness to him in these words:

> I first met Clint Scott when I was a student at the
> Disciples' Eureka College, and Clint was minister of the
> nearby Universalist Church in Peoria, IL. He came to speak
> at the chapel, and he was the first truly liberal minister I
> had ever heard. At that time I didn't know what
> Unitarianism and Universalism were. I questioned him
> afterwards, and I am sure what he said turned me towards
> the liberal ministry . . . Without the creative liberalism of
> Scott there would have been no Meeting House to begin
> with, and without his loyalty and support it would not have
> endured that initial attack, to be able to conduct its exper-
> iments, documented in *A Religion for One World*.(53) Clint
> was a unique person, an ultra-liberal in every sense, who
> yet was droll, patient, gracious, and flexible. He was living
> evidence of one of his books, that religion can make sense.
> Although he supported me and all that I tried to do he
> never tried to steer or coerce the directions that I took. We
> both ignored the attacks and went about our business. By
> the time the controversy ceased being active, the Meeting
> House was five years into its series of projects.(54)

By the mid-1950s the controversy surrounding the Meeting House
had largely subsided, and Patton continued as its minister until 1964,
when he accepted a call to the Unitarian Society of Ridgewood, New
Jersey. The Meeting House never grew to any great size in membership,(55) partly because of its urban location, partly because of its
financial limitations, partly because of its experimental approach to

worship, and partly perhaps because of Patton's personality. After his leaving, the Meeting House underwent a steady decline before closing its doors in the 1970s.

Although it never became the strong center of Universalism that Scott and its other founders envisaged, the Charles Street Meeting House nevertheless made significant contributions to liberal religion. Its chief contributions were, first, the wealth of worship materials—responsive readings, meditations, opening and closing words, and hymn texts—written by Patton and printed and distributed by the Meeting House throughout the denomination; and second, the promotion of the idea of universal religion, a religion for one world, drawing on all sources of religious faith, knowledge, symbolism and practice. If for no other reasons than these the experiment can be judged worthwhile, and Scott deserves major credit both for conceiving the experiment and for seeing that it was carried out. As Kenneth Patton said: "without the creative liberalism of Scott there would have been no Meeting House to begin with, and without his loyalty and support it would not have endured."

But despite the controversies, Scott applied himself to the work of the superintendency with unrelenting vigor and with an unwavering liberal thrust. From time to time he was assisted in his work by a field worker, and always he had an office secretary, but it was essentially a one man operation.(56) In 1951, despite an already heavy work load, he also assumed the superintendency of the Connecticut State Convention, a move that necessitated renaming the *Bay State Universalist* as the *Universalist Trumpet*, since it was to serve both conventions.(57) In addition to his responsibility as Superintendent, Scott began to devote considerable energy to the proposed merger with the Unitarians serving first on the joint Commission on Church Union established in 1950, then on the Council of Liberal Churches (Universalist-Unitarian) and the Joint Interim Committee, both established in 1953. Throughout, he remained a staunch and influential advocate of merger, and in 1955 the joint Interim Committee unanimously recommended that a joint Merger Commission be established to prepare a detailed plan for effecting consolidation.(58) In spite of all these duties, Scott remained at heart very much the parish minister, taking time to make pastoral calls on the residents at the

Doolittle Home for the Aged at Foxboro and on isolated Universalists on Boston's South Shore.(59)

Keeping the pulpits of the churches filled was a never-ending task. Ministers moved often, and in those days there was no elaborate process by which churches searched for replacements. Instead, they usually came directly to the State Superintendent and asked him to recommend someone. The supply of available Universalist ministers was limited, however, and often Scott had to turn to those in fellowship with other denominations, primarily Unitarian or Congregationalist.(60) The Scotts' son Peter, who was also to become a minister, recalls how his father returned to their home in Waltham one evening, announcing with pride and relief that, at last, for the first time in his tenure, every pulpit was filled, only to have the phone ring the next day with the news that a minister had just resigned and a new one was needed!(61)

Scott himself was often out on the road on Sundays, filling vacant pulpits, but this additional task was for him a joy, for he found fulfillment in preaching and missed doing it on a regular basis. The honorarium, when there was one, was always turned over promptly to the Convention Treasurer.(62) Peter recalls an incident relative to these Sunday preaching excursions that illustrated his father's commitment and his mother's self-confidence and practicality. His father had a preaching engagement in Worcester one April Sunday, so Mary drove him to the bus station, her bathrobe over her nightgown and bedroom slippers on her feet. However, when they arrived at the station, they found it was an hour later than they had thought, Daylight Savings Time having started the night before, and the bus had already left. A less committed minister might have phoned the Worcester church with his regrets, and a less self-assured wife might have insisted that he do so; but the preaching engagement was kept, minister speeding off to Worcester in the family car, wife waiting at curb side in her night-clothes to take the city bus back home!(63)

As Superintendent, Scott felt the responsibility to visit as many of the Convention's churches as possible. His record book shows that in his first year, starting with May 1946, he averaged about a dozen such visits a month.(64) He was also called on, in his capacity as Superintendent, to confer ordination on those who had been approved for this by the

Fellowship Committees of the Convention. Thirteen men were thus ordained by Scott, the first three, in 1946 and 1947, being members of the Humiliati—Keith Munson, Earle McKinney and David Cole.(65) A certain amount of controversy surrounded the latter two ordinations, McKinney wearing a stole with the controversial Humiliati symbol of the circle and off-center cross and Cole insisting that he be ordained to the Universalist ministry rather than the Christian ministry, which had been the practice up to that time.(66)

It was through his relationships with the young, liberal ministers and the subsequent influence that these ministers were to have on the Universalist (and, later, Unitarian Universalist) movement, that Scott, in the author's opinion, made his greatest contribution. He guided these ministers, supported them, encouraged them, challenged them, acted as a mentor to them, as "minister to ministers." His son Peter's first wife, Dorothy, summed it up well:

> I do have this sense [about Clint] . . . that it is not the positions he held or the books he wrote that measure his real influence on the denomination. Rather it was in his role as mentor to the men who were young ministers under him when he was superintendent in Massachusetts and Connecticut . . . [who] went on to play important roles in the denomination. I believe that his impact there, though less obvious, was greater and longer-lasting.(67)

These young ministers and their wives and children were always welcome at the Scott home in Waltham, and many of them have warm memories of their visits there with Clinton playing on the floor with the children or telling them stories and Mary making an oyster stew or a batch of raised doughnuts to be served with Vermont maple syrup.(68) When a child was born to one of his protégés, Scott was apt to show up at the door with a present, and several of the male children have "Lee" or "Scott" as one of their names.(69) At the same time, however, he could be a demanding task-master, expecting the same hard work and dedication from the ministers that he required of himself. Earle McKinney, many years later, was to reflect on the way in which state superintendents, and especially Scott, operated:

> Just as they helped [us], the state superintendents could and did lay it on us ministers. And our wives got it from some of the wives of the superintendents. Mary Scott put the "fear of God" in my bride with her expectations of her as a minister's wife. No one would stand for it now; but in those days, respect, awe and love had great weight. Clint Scott was loved and admired and supported by us young ministers; we helped get the Mass. Superintendency for him and held meetings to organize ways his ideas could be adopted.
>
> He appreciated it, but he never relented his basic concept: that the minister was responsible for all the faults of a church . . . Wherever one went in Massachusetts, and for a time Connecticut which Clint also covered, the same cloak of ministerial responsibility would be thrown over one. If the church school wasn't very good it was our responsibility. If the state convention dues were not paid it was the minister's fault. If the church was not growing it was our fault. If someone got angry it was our fault. "God rest your soul, Clint! But you laid a heavy trip on some of us, and it influenced the whole of one's ministry."
>
> If Clint Scott placed a lot of responsibility on us ministers, and we felt it, there was, at least, someone we could support with enthusiasm . . . We had someone who cared what was happening, and what could happen in Massachusetts and in the U.C.A. He gave us a rallying point after Dean Skinner, Al Cole, and others sent us out from Crane with the gospel of Universalism. It had to be proclaimed, and here was our leader.
>
> So while the state superintendents generally felt toward the ministers, "don't you mess up 'my' churches," they also provided the means for us to feel part of a larg-

er movement. We wanted that movement to succeed
through our efforts. We wanted to help Bob Cummins,
Brainard Gibbons and Phil Giles turn the U.C.A. around
and strengthen it, and we did and it did.(70)

Thus Scott, through his leadership, particularly in the influential
Massachusetts Convention, played a major role in liberalizing and
strengthening the Universalist denomination to the point where compatible merger with the Unitarians was possible. While not minimizing the
contributions of Gibbons, Giles and others, it is to Scott, along with
Skinner and Cummins, that the major credit for Universalism's revitalization belongs.(71)

Scott continued working hard right up to the end of his tenure as
Superintendent.(72) On December 28, 1956, a farewell party was held for
Clinton and Mary at the Charles Street Meeting House with many warm
expressions of gratitude and best wishes. Typical was a tribute paid
Clinton by the Reverend Kenneth C. Hawkes, which read in part: "I came
to admire your fairness, caring and sturdy, outspoken liberalism; your
practical, effective churchmanship, and your rare qualities as a solid friend
and minister to ministers."(73)

To all the accolades, Clinton, the consummate storyteller, responded
with a tale about a custodian at a rural Vermont courthouse whose
favorite job was polishing the brass cannon out on the courthouse lawn.
When it finally came time for him to retire, the custodian was asked what
he was going to do with his time, to which he replied, "Well, I'm going to
get my own cannon." "Yep," said Clint, "that's what I'm going to do—get
my own cannon!"(74)

Four days later, on the first of January 1957, Clinton and Mary Scott
were on their way to Tarpon Springs, Florida—Clinton to begin a fourteen year ministry "polishing his own cannon" at the Universalist Church,
Mary to become curator of the church's famous Inness paintings. Thus
Clinton Scott returned to his first and abiding love, the parish ministry,
after a hiatus of eleven years. It was during those eleven years, however,
that he made his most important and lasting contribution to the cause of
liberal religion. The fruits of his labors in Massachusetts are described in

this appraisal of the Convention's 1957 Annual Meeting: "Out of the Convention reports a clear picture of aggressive, liberal churchmanship emerged, in terms of growing churches, new congregations, and imaginative handling of old problems. There is a new tide of confidence, in our movement, and in the special religious insights of Universalism."(75)

Then, just two years later, the merger of the Universalist Church of America and the American Unitarian Association, for which Clinton Scott had helped lay the groundwork and for which he had worked so hard, was voted by overwhelming majorities. The hard work had been worth it.

Notes

1. Peter Lee Scott, "Clinton Lee Scott," Unitarian Universalist Association, Directory, 1987, p. 300.
2. Clinton Lee Scott, *These Live Tomorrow: Twenty Unitarian Universalist Biographies* (Boston: Beacon Press, 1964).
3. For example, Scott is not mentioned either in the text or the biographical appendix of David Robinson, *The Unitarians and the Universalists* (Westport, Conn.: Greenwood Press, 1985) and receives only scant mention in George Huntston Williams, "American Universalism: A Bicentennial Historical Essay," *Journal of the Universalist Historical Society*, Vol. 9 (197 1), or in Elmo Arnold Robinson, *American Universalism: Its Origins, Organization and Heritage* (New York: Exposition Press, 1970). There are numerous scattered references in Russell E. Miller, *The Larger Hope: The Second Century of the Universalist Church in America, 1870–1970* (Boston: U.U.A., 1985), but it is difficult from these to come to an appreciation of Scott's overall influence on the denomination.
4. The churches Scott served were the following: Universalist Church, Northfield, Vermont, 1914–16; Grace Universalist Church, Buffalo, New York, 1916–20; Universalist Church of the Restoration, Philadelphia, Pennsylvania, 1920–23; First Universalist Church, Los Angeles, California, 1923–26; United Liberal Church, Atlanta, Georgia, 1926–30; Universalist Church, Peoria, Illinois, 1930–40; Unitarian Church, Dayton, Ohio, and Universalist Church, Eldorado, Ohio, 1940–42; Independent Christian Church (Universalist), Gloucester, Massachuasetts, 1942–46, Tarpon Springs, Fla, 1957–73.
5. During this controversy Scott was advised by an older minister that, if he were to survive in the ministry, he would have to develop "a hide as tough as a rhinoceros," a piece of advice that he himself was to pass on to young ministers in later years (Clinton Lee Scott, *Some Things Remembered*, Boston: Church of the Larger Fellowship, Unitarian Universalist, 1976, p. 38; letter, Philip R. Giles to author, April

24, 1987). During the Second World War, Scott set aside his pacifism, considering Hitler to be so evil that he had to be stopped (interview with Peter Lee Scott, June 15, 1987).

6. Scott, Some Things Remembered, p. 45.

7. *Ibid.*, pp. 50–51. In response to a smear campaign against Scott by the American Legion, he is reported to have told one of its leaders, "If I hear any more of this, I'm going to kick your ass!" (Letter, Edwin H. Wilson to author: April, 1987).

8. See Scott, *Some Things Remembered*, for an anecdotal account of his life up to this point.

9. Clinton Lee Scott, *Parish Parables* (Boston: Murray Press, 1946).

10. Scott, *Some Things Remembered*, p. 57; author's interview with Gordon McKeeman, June 26, 1987.

11. *Bay State Universalist*, vol 1, No. 2 (Dec. 1946), p. 3.

12. Letter, Clarence R. Skinner to Scott, undated. This and other Scott letters cited are from files in the possession of Peter Lee Scott.

13. *Bay State Universalist*, vol 1, No. I (Sept. 1946), p. 5; vol 1, No. 2 (Dec. 1946), p. 4.

14. *Ibid.*, vol 1, No. 2. p. 8; author's interview with McKeeman.

15. *Bay State Universalist*, vol 1, No. 1, p. 2. The item is unsigned, but Scott later indicated that all unsigned material was written by him. See vol 1, No. 3 (Feb. 1947), p. 8.

16. The Reverend Richard Knost had earlier discovered this symbol at a Universalist society in England, after which he told American Universalists about it; the Humiliati were the first in America to use it in a widespread manner.

17. *Bay State Universalist*, vol 5, No. 3 (Jan. 1951), p. 2.

18. *Ibid.*, vol 1, No. 1, p. 1.

19. *Ibid.*, vol 1, No. 1, p. 2.

20. *Ibid.*, vol 2, No. 1 (Sept. 1947), p. 6.

21. *Ibid.* The first of these appeared in vol 1, No. 2 (Dec. 1946), p. 3.

22. The Larger Fellowship of Universalists was later expanded into a denominational organization which was merged with the Unitarian Church of the Larger Fellowship in 1961. In 1971, this new Church of the Larger Fellowship, Unitarian -Universalist, requested and received Scott's permission to link his name with that of the late Frederick May Eliot in establishing an Eliot-Scott Endowment Fund (Miller, *op. cit.*, pp. 660-661; letter, George Marshall to author, June 5, 1987).

23. *Bay State Universalist*, vol 1, No. 1, p. 3.

24. *Ibid.*, vol 2, No. 1 (Sept. 1947), p. 4

25. Scott, *Religion Can Make Sense* (Boston: Universalist Publishing House, 1949).

26. *Bay State Universalist*, vol 3, No. 3 (Jan. 1949), p. 5. An advantage of the change was the difference in radio voices, Scott's being described as "gravelly," Patton's as "mellifluous" (author's interview with McKeeman).

27. Interview with McKeeman.

28. Scott, *Some Things Remembered*, pp. 46–48; author's interviews with McKeeman and Peter Lee Scott. At the time of the marriage, Mary was better known in the denom-

ination than Clinton, who was often referred to as "Mary Slaughter's husband." Frederick May Eliot, President of the A.U.A., reportedly once said to her during an argument: "Mrs. Scott, you are a very stubborn person!"

29. In addition to serving on the U.C.A. Board for eight years in charge of extension, Mary was heavily involved in the establishment and life of the Charles Street Meeting House, and also served as Associate Editor of the *Bay State Universalist*. The Scott home in Waltham during the years of Clinton's superintendency was always a warm and welcoming place, with many visitors.

30. Miller, pp. 612–623; interview with McKeeman.

31. Miller, p. 618; interview with McKeeman.

32. *Bay State Universalist*, Vol. 5, No. 3 (Jan. 195 1), p. 2.

33. *Ibid.*, vol 3, No. I (Sept. 1948), p. 5; vol 3, No. 3 (Jan. 1949), pp. 6, 7; Roger Etz, vol 3, No. 4 (March 1949), p. 3; Kenneth L. Patton, vol 3, No. 4, p. 4; interview with McKeeman. The date of the service was appropriate, since Ground Hog Day was Scott's favorite holiday. A careful examination of Scott's datebook revales that the memory is faulty. The actual date of Patton's service of installation was Sunday, February 6.

34. Letter to "Fellow Universalists" April 26, 1949.

35. Mary S. Scott to Dorothy Green, March 22, 1950.

36. Dorothy Green to Mary S. Scott, April 5, 1950.

37. In the end, the U.S. Court of Appeals sustained the District Court in dismissing the Convention's suit against station WLAW. Scott thought that the decision was in reaction to Patton's protest at the State House against making Good Friday a legal holiday, and pressure brought by Roman Catholic and Protestant leaders *(Bay State Universalist*, vol 5, No. 1, p. 3). See also, ibid., vol 4, No. 3 (Feb. 1950), p. 6; *Christian Leader*; Feb. 1950, pp. 43 ff; Sept. 1950, pp. 295, 301.

38. Mary S. Scott to Kenneth L. Patton, March 19, 1950.

39. "Criterius," *Christian Leader*, July 1950, p. 232, reprinted in *Bay State Universalist*, vol 5, No. 2 (Nov. 1950), p. 6.

40. Interview with McKeeman.

41. Letter, Gilbert A. Potter to the Churches of the Massachusetts Convention, April 6, 1951.

42. Letter, Kenneth L. Patton to the Universalist Churches of Massachusetts, April 19, 1951.

43. Clinton L. Scott to Chester A. Dunlap, April 12, 1951.

44. Scott to William J. Arms, April 17, 1951; Arms to Scott, April 19, 1951; Scott to Robert Raible, April 17 and April 24, 1951; Scott to Donald King, April 24, 1951; Albert Harkins to Scott, May 31, 1951. Scott had long pushed for such a code of ethical conduct. See *Teamwork*, journal of the Universalist Ministers Association, Oct. 1945, p. 18; Oct. 1948, p. 2; Nov. 1948, p. 8; *Christian Leader*, Oct. 1951, p. 312.

45. Letter to George Spencer, President, Massachusetts Universalist Ministers Association, April 21, 1951.

46. Carl Westman to Scott, April 18, 1951.

47. L. Ronald Kister in "Spendthrift," newsletter of the Swampscott Universalist Church, April 17, 1951.

48. David Hicks MacPherson to Potter, April 12, 1951.

49. See notes 44, 45, 46; also Scott to Westman, April 20, 1951.

50. Letter, Denominational Affairs Committee, Melrose Universalist Church to President and Officers of the State Convention of the Universalist Church of Massachusetts, March 28, 1953.

51. Scott to Horace P. Cutler, Clerk, First Parish in Malden, April 5, 1954.

52. Patton to Scott, January 10, 1952.

53. Patton, *A Religion for One World* (Boston: Beacon Press and Meeting House Press, 1964). For mention of some of the experiments, see *Bay State Universalist*, Vol. 4, No. 2 (Dec. 1949), p. 7; vol 4, No. 3 (Feb. 1950), p. 5; vol 5, No. 2 (Nov. 1950), p. 3.

54. Patton to author, April 14, 1987.

55. There were three classes of membership in the Meeting House: Type A for those with their sole or primary membership there; Type B for those with their primary affiliation elsewhere; and Type C for those outside the Boston area ministered to by radio and mail *(Bay State Universalist*, vol 3, No. 4, March 1949, vol 3, No. 3, Jan. 1949, p. 6.). A membership of 105, including 12 ministers, was reported in February, 1950, Vol. 4, No. 3, Feb. 1950, p. 5). Some of these were probably not Type A members. It is likely that the Type A membership never exceeded 100 (author's interview with McKeeman).

56. George Spencer, Edna Bruner, and Melvin Van de Workeen served as field workers at various times, and Mrs. David Cladwell, Evelyn Sproul, and Mrs. George Young as office secretaries (source: mastheads of *Bay State Universalist* and *Universalist Trumpet*). Barbara Mosher (later Barbara DeWolfe) also worked as an office secretary while a student at Tufts.

57. *Universalist Trumpet*, vol 6, No. I (Sept. 1951), pp. 1–2.

58. *Teamwork*, Nov. 1950, p. 9; Miller, op. cit., pp. 650–652, 656, 724n. Scott, who had held dual fellowship for many years, had been an advocate of merger from at least 1931 (Miller, op. cit., pp. 591, 717n).

59. Aurelie P. Giles to author, April 22, 1987.

60. *Bay State Universalist*, Vol: 2, No. 4 (April 1948), p. 3.

61. Interview with Peter Lee Scott.

62. *Bay State Universalist*, vol 1, No. 2 (Dec. 1946), p. 6.

63. Interview with Peter Lee Scott.

64. Scott's record book indicated the number of such visits. In 1946, they were: May, 11; June, 14; July, 3; August, 3; September, 11. In 1947: January, 11; February, 8; March, 13. Honoraria in 1946: $10, $15, $20, $30. See record book in possession of Peter Lee Scott.

65. Scott's record book lists sixteen such ordinations, but the last three, including that of his son Peter, were after he left the superintendency, and hence were in some

other capacity. Also listed by name, place, and date are 235 christenings, 343 marriages, and 533 funerals.

66. Patricia Bowen, "The Humiliati of Tufts: A Model for Renewal in Religion," D. Min thesis, Meadville/Lombard Theological School, 1978; Miller, op. cit., p. 639.

67. Letter, Dorothy D. Scott to author, June 10, 1987. Specifically mentioned among these young ministers were Ray Hopkins, Bill DeWolfe, Bucky McKeeman, Phil Giles, Ken Patton, and George Spencer. Scott's younger daughter, Martha, recalled the names of "Chuck Reinhardt, Billy DeWolfe, George Spencer, Scotty Meek, Don Lawson, Al and Paul Sawyer, Mel Van de Workeen, Dave and Bob MacPherson, McKeeman, Hayemann—so many young men who would drop by the house, the office, phone, etc." (Martha Scott to author, June 3,1988.) To these could be added David Cole, John Cummins, Bob Dick, Alice Harrison, James Hunt, Earle McKinney, Keith Munson, Albert Niles, Mason McGinness, Carl Westman, Albert Ziegler, and doubtless many others. Many of these ministers rose to positions of denominational leadership.

68. Philip R. Giles to author, April 24, 1987; Susie Giles Godsey to author, April 24, 1987.

69. Interview with McKeeman; letter, George Marshall to author, June 5, 1987.

70. Earle McKinney, "You Are Responsible," Vespers Meditation, 1986 Retreat, Fraters of the Wayside Inn.

71. Gibbons's sermon, "New Wine and Old Bottles," at the U.C.A. biennial in 1947, helped to establish the new "emergent" Universalism as normative, just as Cummins's address at the 1943 biennial had done earlier. Cummins's influence during his long term as General Superintendent, 1938–53, was far greater than that of Gibbons, who served only from 1953 to 1956, or of Giles, who served for the four years leading up to merger, playing a significant role in completing the process. Skinner, through his influential leadership and teaching at Crane from 1911 to 1945, was the chief architect of the new and more inclusive Universalism's theological foundation.

72. Scott's book, *The Universalist Church of America: A Short History* (Boston: Universalist Historical Society, 1957), was completed just before he left the superintendency. The Preface states that a longer, more definitive history was planned by Scott, but it was evidently never written.

73. Hawkes to Scott, Dec. 12, 1956, in a volume of congratulatory letters presented at the party (in possession of Peter Lee Scott); see also *Universalist Trumpet*, vol. 11, No. 4 (March 1957), p. 8.

74. Interview with McKeeman.

75. "The Parish Visitor," newsletter of the Independent Christian Church (Universalist), Gloucester, Mass., late May issue, 1957. The author was probably Walter Royal Jones, the church's minister.

Chapter 5

That Controversial Sermon:
The Prostitution of the Clergy

Kenneth L. Patton

(Delivered at the Charles Street Meeting House, Sunday, February 11, 1951)

The word "prostitution" is derived from a Latin word, "prostitutus," meaning "placed before, exposed publicly." In its most common usage it refers to a woman who sells her body, but in general terms it refers to any activity in which something which would not ordinarily be considered for sale is put to hire. It is in this sense that a minister is a prostitute, for he earns money in the performance of his religion. A person's religion is considered to be the most intimate, personal, and profound range of his life. That religious devotions should be exhibited in public to earn a salary is perhaps as inherently disgraceful as the public performance of the sex act for a fee, but custom has blinded us to this obvious prostitution. Perhaps because the minister is credited with being a professionally virtuous man, and it does not readily occur that putting virtue to hire is as debasing as putting something that has been considered sinful to hire.

The evil of all prostitution ensues from the degrading of person and character when the most worthful experiences are sold in order to attain something less worthful. When the standards of value in which we believe are disarranged, the mainstays of our personalities collapse. Only when we hold to that which is precious even though we must sacrifice lesser goods do we add strength and fiber to our moral determination and habits. Perhaps we must always let these carry with them their own inherent rewards, and never let them become the vehicles through which we earn money, or attain prestige, or satisfy ambition. For if we let them become involved with lesser goals, we may be tempted to use them as means to lesser ends, and thus prostitute them.

The Quakers have been one of the few religious groups to be sensitive to the danger of prostitution in a "hireling clergy." John W. Graham speaks for them when he points out "that all attempts to work a spiritual communion on commercial principles are likely to end in perverting the spiritual into the type of the economic . . . the inner mind of the preacher is altered by the intrusion of the professional spirit and the professional fee." He points out that ministers "are under servitude. . . . For they are bound to be popular, not only because their living is at stake, but because their whole sphere of usefulness goes with it. [*The Faith of a Quaker,* John W. Graham, Cambridge University Press, 1930].

Graham puts his finger upon the essential danger of prostitution in being a religious professional. "Again all preaching which counts, means that a man unbares his soul. His deep religious experience, his most private self is exhibited for the help of others. This is, indeed, in itself a glorious function—this is the true priestly act, communicating divine things. But to exploit your personality like this for a living! I don't like the idea, and the true and honest preacher forgets it if he can."

If he can—but he cannot. The fact of his prostitution dogs and haunts him, and causes him to doubt his own motives in every performance of his religious function. What is the *real* reason I am doing this? Would I do this in just this way if my professional life did not depend on it? Am I preaching this because I believe it, or because the people want it, and I want to keep my job? Am I nice to this person because I want to be nice, or because it is my trade? A sophisticated minister who knows how easily men can delude themselves knows it to be impossible to make a simple answer to such questions.

Religious prostitution is as old as organized religion itself. One of the earliest functions of the temple was to serve as a brothel for the religious prostitutes. The fact that the living of the priests depended on the religious giving and sacrifices of the people has for millennia contributed to the corruption of the priesthood. The performance of rites and sacraments, the propitiation of the gods through prayers and magic offered temptations to profit and power that not even the supposed sanctity of the clergy could resist. Modern churches and their ministry are far from free of this ancient pollution.

Inherent in this whole problem is the conflict between the aims and necessities of personal faith as against the aims and necessities of institutional religion. The young minister is confronted with this issue from the first moment he considers entering the ministry. His attraction to this profession is largely to derive from his highest ideals and finest sensibilities. A life spent in the study and contemplation of religious ideas and goods, to spend one's whole effort in the promotion of a better world, the chance to serve and guide the people, this holds a strong appeal for the adolescent idealist.

If one were to follow that beckon, he must keep himself free, free from the secondary and sordid attractions that engulf so many people in a pursuit of pleasure and materialistic profit. He must keep his mind free from all slaveries, in order that he may make honest judgements and speak them without favor. He must keep his emotions and loyalties free from attachments that might entice him away from dedication to his high purposes. It is this struggle of personal conscience against the rewards of servitude to the world that is pictured in the story of the period spent by Jesus in the wilderness at the beginning of his ministry. And it is not without point that Jesus remained free only by working outside of, and often against, the established religion of his people.

The young neophyte clergyman goes to seminary, and there he finds little encouragement to develop a personal faith and conviction based on his own insights, judgments, and feelings. Rather he is used like an empty vessel, as a handy container into which the already-prepared theology and practice of the church can be dumped. If he has a religion when he arrives, his teachers try to rid him of it, as they might pull a bad tooth. He is treated as a religious ignoramus whom it is their commission to train and enlighten. He is eviscerated like a chicken, stuffed with dressing made to the proper theological recipe, and then placed in the ovens of the churches he serves, and after a few years of roasting, if he has pleased the judicious eyes of the several cooks, he is given a big church and is devoured down to his bones by his rapacious congregations. And, to change the metaphor back to our original one, he resembles nothing so much as a high-priced harlot that has undergone a successful apprenticeship, and is properly installed in a costly apartment for an appreciative trade.

His fate becomes apparent when he applies for his first pulpit. The indignities visited upon a minister when he candidates for a church are the bane of all ministers who have scruples and sensitivities other than those of a salesman. He is placed on inspection, quizzed as to his religious convictions, judged as to the pleasingness of his personality, given trial to see if he can pray and preach with proper orthodoxy and power, entertained in several homes to judge his table manners and his household habits, watched to see if he has a way with old ladies and children and whether he is popular with youth, his wife is microscopically examined to see if she measures up to the proper standards of a "minister's wife." He begins to wonder if they wait until he laughs to get a good look at his teeth.

It is in the experiencing of all of these various considerations as to his adequacy as a minister that the young clergyman begins to appreciate that other factors are operating rather than the principles and ideals that he has envisioned in the "high calling." For if ministers are prostitutes, the fault at least in part lies with the congregations that are so insistent upon making prostitutes out of them. A people that properly appreciated freedom of religious belief and action would not insist on making their preachers mere parrots of their prejudices and the time-servers of their whims. If they are in turn used by preachers who have learned the tricks of their trade and know how to charm and titillate their customers, they are only getting the treatment they have demanded and deserve. For the penalties of a free and courageous voice in the pulpit are almost incredible when compared with the vaunted ideals espoused as the nature of religious faith and practice. It is the Jesus "meek and mild" that the minister is supposed to emulate, not the Jesus whose outspoken mission got him hung in some six months or three years, depending on the scholar you read, but not a long pastorate in either case. It is probably impossible to find a greater disparity than the standards of Jesus' ministry and those of the hireling clergy. The Quakers saw this clearly and quoted Jesus, along with Amos and the other prophets, in their attacks upon the professional ministry.

Perhaps this evil is of the very nature of institutions, and religion and both the ministers and the members will undergo both subtle and obvious disintegration whenever institutions are used for embodiment and expression. For the institution, with its powers and prestige, becomes an end in itself, and the principles and aims of religious idealism are sacrificed to feed the maw of the church. This is indicated in the title of "churchman" given to a minister, which means that he is a good servant of the church as an institution. Success is judged, not according to the promotion of religious ideals, but according to the membership, budget, building facilities, and busywork of the church organization. That it is possible to have a large and prosperous institutional structure without any essentially religious function does not seem to occur to those involved, for the church has become the end in itself, and not a means to higher ends, and the preacher has become its organizer, its front man.

This is of the very nature of prostitution. Sex, like worship, is elevating only when it serves the highest needs and goals of human personality. It deteriorates as soon as it is divorced from an expression of love, respect, and companionship between a man and a woman. It suffers when it bears no relation to the bearing of children as the act through which the wonder of life is continued. It suffers as soon as it is separated from the full and various life of the family, and is made an end in itself apart from other interests and activities. Above all it is debased when it is made an instrument of lust on the part of the man, and an instrument of greed and profit on the part of the prostitute.

When religion is set aside from the rest of life within the church, as sex is set aside in the brothel, it degenerates. It becomes an end in itself, rather than a mood, a set of principles and ideals that live only as they are applied to everyday living. There is no real religion except as it is applied in the marketplace, in the home, in the school, in the shop, on the streets.

Shut apart from life in the musty gloom of the church it becomes inbred, diseased, effete. Its practice becomes a kind of religious lust, indulged in for its own fetid and self-defeating pleasures. And the minister becomes the professional who runs the house and organizes the debaucheries.

Perhaps only the preacher can be aware of the changes that occur in himself and in his religion when he makes the expression of his belief and faith an object of barter. For the preacher has certain commodities for sale, as does any other businessman—certain skills, services, and artifacts. As an amateur he would express his religious views without any consideration other than to make himself understood. Ordinarily he would say what he thought regardless of whether his opinions pleased another or made him friends and influenced people. We have made it a principle in this country that a man's religion is his own affair and that it shall not be a consideration in his fitness for a job or a public office. This we have made a matter for law. In this setting we have a very healthy frankness and fearlessness in the belief and practice of religion.

Except in the clergy—for here is one profession where the nature of religious convictions is considered of prime importance in fitness for hiring. It is inevitable that the preacher begins to consider his statements of faith, not only in terms as to whether they project his honest beliefs, but in terms of their salability to those who are buying them. This is called "beginning with the people where they are," or speaking to them in relation to their own experience and in words they can comprehend. But it also means, in practice, telling them only what they will like in the way that they will like it. Many ideas and topics are shelved because they would be distasteful to this member or that or would be unfitted to the "dignity of the pulpit." The minister has become an actor in a role concerned with the box office appeal of his performance.

This being the case, he presents only a thin, dehydrated slice of life, for, like the movie producer, he has his "Hays Office" with its censorship rulings to which he must conform or meet official displeasure. The rich and vulgar pageant of life churns about him, but he may treat only certain trite and prettied aspects of it. There is a tacit "editorial policy" that operates as an automatic censorship on the content of church services, as surely as it works to shape the content of a newspaper, magazine, or movies This makes all of them inadequate interpreters of the whole of life, mirrors which reflect back only a dim, blurred, and contorted picture of man and his world.

It is inevitable that in time his religious emotions, mannerisms, ways of thought, principles, and personality should take on the aura and shape of the institutionalized religion he purveys. Instead of being a creative, generating, original religious force, he is a lifeless puppet jerked around by the unseen wires of habit and conformity. His posturing and antics are stale repetitions, without native passion and original force. He speaks not his own words, but the words of the prayer book, hymnal, scripture and theological tract. These are the cold, sterile acts of the paid performer, who does the expected thing in the expected ways, showing forth a mask on which is painted an attitude of devotion and sanctification, which hide a thoughtless emptiness of boredom within. The performance of excitement and satisfaction are also present in the religious prostitutes, whether the reality is there or not, for the patron must be convinced that he is being properly served. The prostitution of the clergy is an even more profound and corrupting prostitution than that of the harlot, for whereas it is her physical body that she sells, it is what might be called his "spiritual body" that the minister offers for hire.

It is in his human relations that the minister is most deeply deranged. Like the professional actor, he begins to wonder when he is reacting sincerely and when he is just performing a role. He develops a counterpart of the doctor's "bedside manner," a ministerial pose of blithe and hearty optimism which is often used as a shield to cover the true nature of his feelings and his true judgement as to the seriousness of his patients'— that is, his parishioners'—state of health. Whereas any small delinquency on his part, if known by his parish, would be cause for his removal, as a pastoral counselor he becomes the depository for the sins of his people, both large and small. This always receiving confidences but never giving them, because of fear of consequences, unbalances the equality of the give and take of human relations. At its worst he becomes a moral snob, since he thinks himself able to give advice, but does not feel that he needs it. At its best it leaves a very lonely person, for though he must always be ready to let others unload their woes upon him, he has no ears for his own troubles that he can trust. Many ministers find relief from this isolation through personal friends outside their own congregation or among their colleagues. But there is something inherently wrong with a situation that necessitates this amputation of normal human intercourse.

His human relations are further troubled because his relation to people is ambivalent. He may like a person, but his motives in approaching this person are always suspect. For he depends on the massing of people for his support, Like the politician, any overtures he makes may be judged as an attempt to win another vote. Is he promoting this person for membership, for another "star" in his professional "crown?" Is he trying to add to his professional prestige through another face in the Sunday morning congregation? Is his preaching and praying the expression of sincere emotions or mere exhibitionism? Is his whole ministerial function motivated by devotion to a high cause, or just the outlet of a personal success drive? Does he smile and "glad hand" the people because he enjoys them, or is he buttering them up for a contribution? Is he objective and impartial in his thinking and preaching, or is he trying to enforce the domination of his religious ideas on his audience? Did he enter the ministry for sincere reasons, or because it gave him a ready role for his self-righteous boorishness? Is he a minister in order to serve the people, or in order to enforce his belief in his religious superiority?

The people sense the falseness of their human relations with the minister. If the minister has a pulpit personality for their consumption, they have a "pose of religiosity" for his sake. Rather than acting as they would in a normal situation, they act as they think the preacher would expect them to act. The pose is a sham from both sides, The minister must act as if he is more moral and more easily shocked than other mortals, but he knows that he is not, and so do the people. Yet they seem to be pleasantly surprised to discover that a preacher can act like a human being. This is his penalty for allowing himself to be set apart. But there are ministers who enjoy the role, who like to be called "reverend," and who actually look upon themselves as being in some unique fashion a "man of God." And there are people who insist that their ministers shall assume this dishonest role. Again, it takes two parties to make prostitution.

Since he must please the people in order to strengthen the institution he serves, the minister hedges his bets, shies away from unpopular causes, keeps a "yes and no" answer ready for awkward situations. He becomes "all things to all men," which is a perfect description of the behavior of the prostitute. His function is to win over, not to instruct, to shock or to move to radical convictions and actions. He must give no offense to individuals, to institutions, to the state, to business, or even to other religious groups. If the church endangers their respectability the people may consider it a luxury they cannot afford. He must keep his house from becoming notorious in the community. Graham comments on this need to be popular. "That is why the testimony of the Churche— say on War—is never above, and often below, that of the average good man. Nor can this be avoided so long as the system is retained. What a twist this need for popularity gives to the single eye." It leads the followers of "the Prince of Peace" to become camp followers, blessing the carnage and praying for the success of arms. To say nothing about keeping track of the boys while they are away from home and making sure they will be good church members if and when they come back.

Most churches serve only a narrow stratum of the population, whether it be a middle class group, a society group, a working man's church, or a white church, or a colored church. If the minister is to expect success, he must learn to echo the prejudices of the social class he serves, live according to the style of his group, and offend none of their shibboleths. He is as much a paid servant at the disposal of his masters as is a butler or maid.

One of the major evils of prostitution is that it is parasitical, performing no useful function other than satisfying certain desires at convenient times. Novels of houses of prostitution picture them as places of boredom and ultimate meaninglessness. The church and the minister are often such parasites upon the active community. Churches are cannibalistic, feeding upon their own flesh, living merely to continue their own existence. Their only appeals to the community are for attendance at their events and contributions for their budgets. The church is to be served, not to serve. The people are concerned with their own religious adornment, with the gratification of their pious feelings, with the satisfaction of their habitual and conditioned religious practices. They have somehow concluded that a church is good for the community whether it does anything to justify that reputation or not, merely because it is a church. The minister often gets the same pleasant delusions about himself.

What is the minister to do? He can either leave the ministry, perhaps only to find himself involved in some other professional prostitution. Or he may decide to stay in his role but struggle against it and determine not to like it. But if he does the latter, he should be warned that the inroads of corruption are insidious and subtle, and if the prostitution inherent in his role is too fundamental and powerful there is no way that he can prevail against it in the long run. Must we take the Quaker alternative and have no professional clergy, to let every man be his own preacher without pay? Graham makes the potent observation that "The peculiarity of the Society of Friends is not that there is no clergy; it is that there is no laity."

Implied in what we have been considering is the even more serious problem of what this does to the people, who let the performance of the minister be a vicarious religious experience for them, taking a fan role rather than being the creators and effectors of their own religious practice. The patrons of the prostitute degrade themselves, using her as a substitute for an adequate emotional adjustment and maturity in their own personality. Insofar as the minister is a prostitute, he likewise injures those who support and use him. And, after all, if the minister is a prostitute, what does that make of the church?

Section II

Personal Stories

Chapter 6

Growing Up with the Charles Street Meeting House

Peter Lee Scott

This paper represents a particular approach to historical research—with the historian as participant. I share with you accounts and insights coming from five sources:

1. My own participation as one of the founding members of the Charles Street Universalist Meeting House.
2. Anecdotal material, especially from my parents, Clinton Lee Scott and Mary Slaughter Scott.
3. Writings of Kenneth L. Patton
4. Other publications, especially that of the *Bay State Universalist* and the *Universalist Trumpet.*
5. Unpublished correspondence relating to the Meeting House from my parents' files.

It is a pleasure to me to present this paper; it has meant retracing many steps from one of the most interesting periods of our recent history. I make three initial observations.

1. In terms of building a viable congregation in Boston, Kenneth L. Patton had the field of liberal religion to himself for many years—and he blew it!

2. In terms of effecting a pilot project in Universalism, Ken provided the focal point for the left wing of the Universalist denomination and the growing edge of the faith. His work was instrumental in winning through to the clear understanding that Universalism is not limited to theism or to Christianity.

3. And in providing us with a body of philosophy, poetry, hymnology and worship materials, Ken Patton indeed gave us a lasting legacy—the symbolism, setting, and writing for naturalistic mysticism, for the neo-Pagan side of our religion, for a religion of one world.

I was in the eighth grade in the spring of 1947 when plans were made to start a new Universalist Church in Boston. Delegates to the Massachusetts Universalist Convention at its convention that May recommended that "we endorse and encourage the establishing of a Universalist Church in the city of Boston." It is fair to say that most of them had no real idea of where this vote would take them.

My father, Clinton Lee Scott, had been since 1946 state superintendent for the Massachusetts Universalist Convention. Under his leadership, the decline of Universalism in Massachusetts was halted and new growth began, the MUC changed from being the center of conservative Universalism to the growing edge of liberal Universalism, and younger, more liberal ministers were encouraged to settle there and were supported in their work by the superintendent. The pages of the Convention magazine regularly reported the ordinations of young ministers coming to Massachusetts and Connecticut churches, their marriages, and the birth of their children.

With the revitalization of the MUC and Universalism in the state, there was a strong feeling that we should again have a Universalist church in Boston. At least 20 Universalist churches had existed in Boston in past years, the last new one founded in 1893. The only remaining ones, East Boston and Grove Hall Church in Dorchester, were on their last legs.

The initial intent in Boston was to start a new church that would be a "pilot project in Universalism," deliberately on the growing left edge of the denomination, in effect a flagship church for the MUC in the city of Boston.

As a 13-year-old kid, I was not central to this planning, but being in the family and a committed Universalist, I was, in effect, a part of it right from the start.

Dr. Roger Etz was president of the Convention and worked hard to bring this new church into existence. The board of the MUC unanimously supported the Convention's vote, and the first step was to find a building. The one we found, the Charles Street Meeting House, on the corner of Charles and Mt. Vernon Streets, was originally built in 1805 as the Third Baptist Church at the edge of the Charles River so as to be able conveniently to perform baptisms.

John G. Green, of the Society for the Preservation of New England Antiquities, was instrumental in our getting this building. The MUC bought it on June 28, 1948. There had been many owners and tenants over the years, including the AME Church and the Albanian Eastern Orthodox Church just before us.

During the summer of 1948 plans were made for renovation and decoration of the building. My father and I cleaned out the stuff left behind as the previous church vacated the premises. A painted crucifix ended up planted in our compost heap in Waltham, Massachusetts.

Herman Gutheim led in the initial work of redecorating the building. Harry Adams Hersey reconditioned three pianos for the church. Grove Hall and East Boston Universalist churches contributed needed furniture. Donald MacMillan of Weymouth helped get a Universalist Unitarian college-age group organized.

There was lots of discussion about what to name the church. We'd had First, Second, etc., in Boston. Someone suggested we call it "The Last Universalist Church in Boston." (And it turned out that it *was* that.) The Charles Street Universalist Meeting House name was finally chosen both to play on the historic, traditional setting and to take a name that was deliberately nonecclesiastical.

In the fall of 1948 the building was put into use, with the Greater

Boston Universalist Ministers meeting there (with Clarence Skinner and Alfred Cole as program chairs), and with a Saturday educational program that had persons such as Clyde Kulckhohn of Harvard working with it.

Clinton Lee Scott was the first member of the congregation in the fall of 1948. There was a 200% increase the second day as Peter Lee Scott and Mary Slaughter Scott then joined.

Three types of membership were established:

A. Primary affiliation for those in or near Boston.
B. For those in or near Boston affiliated with another church but desiring to be identified with and give support to the Meeting House.
C. For isolated Universalists in places where there was no Universalist church.

Calling a minister was the next order of business. The Convention Board of Trustees asked the Superintendent to recommend a minister. Dr. Etz writes in the *Bay State Universalist* that many ministers were considered for the position, though naturally he does not list names.

I know personally that Horton Colbert, Minister of the Universalist church in Rochester, Minnesota, was the first actually chosen for Minister of Charles Street. He was a strong preacher, a caring pastor, a scholar and student of Far Eastern religions, and he had a good record at building churches. He and his family moved east from Rochester to take the job. They had a daughter a year younger than I was (the Rev. Carolyn Colbert, today), and two younger, adopted children. One was black, and because of this they had immediate difficulty finding anyone willing to rent or sell them a house. They lived for over a year with us in Waltham, until they finally found a house in Lexington.

Right after they arrived in Massachusetts, the position of Director of the Department of Education of the Universalist Church of America came open and Horton was needed there. He became Director of that department and we went looking for another minister.

Kenneth L. Patton was the next choice after Horton Colbert. Ken, a former Disciples of Christ minister turned Unitarian, had made a name for himself in Madison, Wisconsin from 1942 to 1948. His preaching was outstanding; he had become nationally known for his remark, on radio, that he would like to resign from the white race to join the human race. He had also been instrumental in bringing the Madison congregation and the famed architect, Frank Lloyd Wright, together. He was 37 years old when he came to Boston. To the best of my knowledge the decision to call him was made by Clinton Lee Scott, with Horton Colbert joining in to persuade Patton to move. It took two rounds of persuasion to get Patton to consider leaving Madison.

By November 1948 Ken had been formally and unanimously called by the Massachusetts Universalist Convention Board, after he had an earlier long and detailed meeting with that board. There was no congregational call, as the congregation had not yet begun to function.

At that meeting with the MUC board, Patton spelled out very thoroughly what he intended to do with the Meeting House project. There were many questions and lots of discussion. It was agreed that the project would take from five to ten years to fulfill.

Clinton Scott wrote that the deliberate task of the Meeting House was to "be an experimental station or laboratory for discovering and developing ways to meet the needs and the opportunities of the new age." Patton wrote, "Part of the reason I came to the Meeting House to head up a 'pilot project' was curiosity. It seemed too good to be true. It was. But it did let the camel get his nose in the tent. For a camel to be established in an old Meeting House in the center of Boston is certainly one of the oddest spectacles in human history."

Patton was installed as Minister at a service on February 6, 1949. Dr. Etz headed the Installation committee. The church was filled for the service. Music came from the choir of the Universalist Church in Lynn. Sunday services began the next week.

When Patton began there was an immediate groundswell of enthusiasm. Large congregations were present at services from the start. On Easter Sunday of 1949 I was one of the ushers. I remember well the decision that the ushers finally made to open the balcony despite fire laws against its use; we filled the balcony and had standing room only that day.

In that beginning period lots of folks dropped in to see what was happening. A fair number joined immediately, 44 in the first month. Charles Street became the fastest-growing church in Massachusetts Universalism; there were 105 members by the end of the first year and over a dozen ministers were among that membership.

Ken Patton had the field to himself. All the Unitarian churches in Massachusetts were conservative. Many of the Universalist ones were also. There was a new liberal, humanist element among the Universalists, but obviously not in Boston itself.

Patton took uncompromising positions right from the start. For example, at his installation service, he refused to wear a robe, even after a direct request from Clinton Lee Scott that he do so. In the pulpit Ken regularly wore a business suit that rode up over his rear end.

He got into controversy early on. The MUC radio broadcasts are an example. Clinton Lee Scott and others had been speaking on station WLAW since September 30, 1946. There had been no problems and there was a wide listening audience of both Universalists and others. Patton took over the program starting January 2, 1949, and was thrown off the air by Easter! The station asked for his Easter script in advance, a first-time request. Patton intended to say, "Did Jesus rise from the dead? We do not know." Clinton Scott had flatly stated the previous year that the resurrection was a myth. But Patton had a week or so earlier said, "Jesus was the kind of fellow who, when the party ran dry, would go around the corner for another case of beer." The real offense was not so much *what* he said, but *how* he said it. Also the station said it canceled "because of protests from our listeners" and these, though never proven, were probably from conservative Universalists who had been urged to pressure the station.

Another example of deliberate provocation was Ken's publicly refusing to pay his income tax just before Betty was to have their fifth child, which would have removed the family from a category that owed any taxes at all.

Patton attracted people in droves by what he was doing at the Meeting House, and then drove them away almost as fast by the roughness of his personality. He had a magnetic strength that was not at all affected, but some deliberate effort to be nice to people would have helped.

He was a powerful preacher, very straightforward in his speaking. His sermons read as well as he preached them. He preached always from manuscript and had his sermons duplicated for distribution. He believed in getting maximum mileage from his work. He once told me of an address he'd written which, with some rewriting, he managed to use in a half dozen places within a year.

He was a good teacher in small adult classes—lucid, insightful, open to discussion, open to other's ideas. My interest in classical Taoism dates from one such class.

The Charles Street Meeting House should have become one of our biggest churches. Instead, it never grew in membership to a self-supporting level. Its maximum membership was around two hundred.

With the Universalist Unitarian Consolidation, the MUC went out of business and its support of the budget ended. Eventually, in 1964, Patton left to go to serve the Unitarian Church in Ridgewood, New Jersey, just to earn a living. He continued to serve Charles Street on a part-time basis with Alan Seaburg as co-minister until 1968.

While Kenneth L. Patton was the focal point of the Meeting House, the real founder of it was Clinton Lee Scott. Scott continued to be an active member of it, along with his wife, Mary Slaughter Scott, and son, Peter Lee Scott. Clinton Scott served as its protector as well, from 1949 through 1956, shielding it from attacks that otherwise would have been fatal. The MUC office in January 1953 moved from 16 Beacon Street to the Meeting House, both to save on rent and to stress the partnership between the convention and the church.

Charles Howe in his article on Clinton Scott implies that Patton lost the support of Mary Scott, stating that she became exasperated with Patton, and he tied this to "opposition rising" in the MUC. The fact is that while my mother certainly did get exasperated with Ken regularly, and told him so privately in a letter dated March 19, 1950, her public support for him and the Meeting House never wavered.

The Meeting House became the focal point for conservative opposition to Clinton Scott and his liberalization of the Massachusetts and Connecticut conventions. Scott would have had a far easier time as state superintendent if it had not been for Ken Patton. Patton and the Meeting

House were under constant attack from 1949 on, and the Convention's budget suffered badly when several of the conservative churches withheld payment of their fair share.

The annual Massachusetts conventions became the battleground over the Meeting House and the new Universalism. On April 26, 1949, a letter signed by six Universalists ministers (William Wallace Rose, Frank Chatterton, Arthur Webster, Leslie Nichols, John Wood and Charles Monbleau) sent to all ministers in the MUC said they were deeply troubled over the MH being a stronghold of humanism, "outside the Christian frame of reference." Clinton Lee Scott wrote: "They were genuinely concerned that the Charles Street Church was sponsoring religious ideas inconsistent with a type of Universalism that was Christian and theistic. They were right: it was."

Some of the objection was to Patton's sermon titles, for example, "Upsadaisy" at Easter, and "I Should be in Jail" (about the Massachusetts anti-blasphemy law). The opposition agreed that he should be in jail, and they were outraged at the sermon ad in the Boston papers. The unhappiness over ads for Patton's sermons run in Boston newspapers was that these were giving the public the impression that Universalism was humanistic and concerned with universal religion, things that Patton had been the very direct about with the convention board.

One minister, Gilbert Potter of Fitchburg, took a sermon of Ken's ("The Prostitution of the Clergy"), had it reprinted (without permission) and sent it out across the state as a horrible example of what we were paying for. This action was taken without concern for ministerial ethics, legal concerns, freedom of the pulpit or congregational polity. Ken was not regarded by opposing ministers as a fellow Universalist.

It should be noted that most Universalist ministers in Massachusetts supported Patton and went to bat for him. The opposition was a minority one, though strong. The outcry against Potter's action was immediate and loud, and came not just from Massachusetts but from across the country. Further, the MUC Board, though it tended to be generally conservative in nature, continued its support of Patton and the Meeting House until merger ended the MUC.

This was the main battleground between conservatives and liberals within Universalism. It became the symbolic battle and one where conservatives were fighting hard to retain their hold on the denomination. The fought hard because they knew they were losing.

The Massachusetts Universalist Fellowship Committee, headed (I think) at that time by Albert Ziegler, refused to grant fellowship to either the congregation or to Patton, on the grounds that he and it were not really Universalist, even while the MUC paid the bills and owned the property. The issue then went to the floor of the convention four years in a row.

In the convention debates Patton was no help whatsoever to his own cause, in effect telling the delegates to go to blazes. His was neither a moderate nor a conciliatory voice. While these battles tend to run together in my memory, I recall the first one, 1949, where Meeting House members representing both Charles Street and the defunct Grove Hall Dorchester Church, both delegates and alternates, got away with voting on whether or not they were to have a vote.

At a convention in Wesley I spoke as a theological student, noting the number of students at St. Lawrence who were humanist or universalist in belief. The next day back in Canton, New York, I was called on the carpet by Dean Angus MacLean—"Now what have you been up to?" News of my speech had reached Canton before I had, and reprisals had been threatened to the SLU Building Campaign (from Universalist Churches in Salem, Lynn, and Malden, I believe). Those churches had long since cut off the MUC from their support, but their threats to St. Lawrence were never carried through.

In the heat of debate one year at a convention held in Worcester, Clinton Scott rose to speak in defense of the Meeting House, but found he had completely lost his voice. At lunchtime, when he had gone one block away from the church his voice returned. It disappeared on his return to the convention floor, reappeared later a block away, etc. for the rest of the day.

One year a roll call of delegates was called for on the Charles Street issue, prompting the showing of individual colors on the issue. Early on, the Rev. Weston Cate loudly voted "No", followed immediately by Arlene Cate glaring at her husband, even more loudly declaring "Yes!" Thankfully this produced a round of laughter.

In 1949, meeting in Cambridge, the convention denied fellowship to Charles Street. In 1950, at Malden, again fellowship was not granted and while that year the conservatives had the votes to close down the Meeting House they deliberately held off, hoping to gain even more strength the next year. But in 1951, with a conservative move to cut the Meeting House out of the MUC budget, the liberals were better organized; they kept it in the budget, and elected a new board of trustees to the convention board and Alan Sawyer, Sr. as convention president. Then in 1952 fellowship was finally granted.

Music was important at the Meeting House. The first choir director was an old Boston Unitarian. As a professional musician he went along with Ken Patton, but he was a bit aghast at him. I sang in the choir. The choir loft was in the rear of the sanctuary. I used to read Ken's (printed) sermons ahead of time and then played solitaire during their preaching. The director firmly asked that I cease this.

Ken had a highly involved liturgical service, with lots of choir participation. One Sunday morning a snow storm kept the choir at home save for me and one alto. She refused to sing, so I sang the entire service, in effect doing a duet with Patton.

Ken thought if he could sing something (at all) then it was singable for the choir. He was known for putting the empHASis on the wrong sylLABLE. I got him to admit defeat once—that they had indeed included at least one unsingable hymn in *Hymns for the Celebration of Life* ("Now in the Tomb is Laid").

Patton's work on the Commission that produced *Hymns for the Celebration of Life* was important denominationally. The book was a big step forward, including a large amount of humanistic/naturalistic material. Ken's influence was significant in including readings and hymns from outside the Judeo-Christian tradition. Much of that hymnal came out of the Charles Street Meeting House; many of the hymns and responsive readings were from Ken himself.

I regularly took part in work-nights at the Meeting House. At them, all kinds of things were going on at once: sweeping the floors, putting loose-leaf hymnals together, printing always, carpentry and metalwork, photography, organ installation (putting two of them together), choir rehearsal, plus good food and fellowship.

There was a strong and dedicated core of loyal members who stuck by the place over the years. See especially Alan Seaburg's article for his tribute to them.

The Meeting House Press was an early development and perhaps the longest lasting one. (As Carl Braden used to say, in a version of A. J. Leibling's adage: "Freedom of the press exists for those who have a press.") At first there was a mimeograph machine, then a small press for pamphlets, then a larger, more modern one. It was never "state of the art," but it kept producing. If Ken had had today's computer typesetting and copier technology there's no end to what he would have produced. Corliss Lamont of New York City was of great help in underwriting the printing program.

Overall, Kenneth Patton pretty much ran the show himself. It was his show. He had conceived it, defended it and labored for it. Only occasionally did he back down versus someone. One instance that I recall involved him and Mary Scott—over an African mask he had hung up in the dining hall. Mary said, "Not where I have to look at it when I'm eating dinner."

Ken had the enthusiastic support of his congregation—those who stayed with him. The attacks on the Meeting House and its minister strengthened the bonds of unity. At one point he opposed their support of his going to Ridgewood, New Jersey. Ken announced that he'd be going there part time and continuing part time at the Meeting House. At a congregational meeting I moved that we approve this. Ken opposed my motion on the grounds that all the congregation could do was to call him or fire him; what he did as minister was totally up to himself. The motion remained and was passed by the meeting despite Ken's unhappiness over support he hadn't asked for and didn't want.

Ken could be and often was utterly ruthless in argument. He is the only person I've seen best Rabbi Sherwin Wine in a debate, which he did thoroughly at a national Fellowship of Religious Humanists convention. But this ability unfortunately got used on quite ordinary folks all the time.

Ken was a loner, and was himself lonely. He had hundreds of followers and still has today, but I don't think he had many friends. Aside from Vincent Silliman, I'm not sure who he felt close to personally.

Clinton Lee Scott had his respect and gratitude, but they were not close personally. I was a kid growing up in his church. I considered him my minister and mentor, but not a personal friend. In 1963 I exchanged pulpits with him from the Melrose Unitarian church and he told me that was the only pulpit exchange he'd been offered in fourteen years in Boston!

In a letter to my father in 1952, Ken said, "I'm a stubborn bastard, if nothing else. I'll make this thing go, or I'll die trying." I hope Ken had some idea of how much his material came to be used in our denomination, (quoted more than Jesus, I suspect, and to better purpose), but he felt himself rejected both by the denomination (which he had little use for) and by his fellow ministers.

After Ken moved south, the congregation continued with the co-ministry and then the ministry of the Rev. Alan Seaburg, and then faltered badly under subsequent leadership. The art project was "looted" (Ken's term), and the symbols finally ended up at Starr King School for The Ministry in Berkeley.

The new thrust to Universalism as a religion for one world, which was gaining rapid success within the UCA, died out after merger when our total emphasis became one of "freedom."

A strong attempt was made in 1979 to persuade the UUA Board to revive and keep the Meeting House going, but this fell on deaf ears, and the UUA eventually sold the building for $225,000. The sanctuary was gutted in 1980, replaced by commercial activities. But the effect of the Meeting House project upon the denomination(s) has gone far beyond the continuation of one congregation. It stands as one of the landmark churches of the Universalist tradition, and through Kenneth L. Patton's writings it will continue to affect our faith.

Bibliography

Patton, Kenneth L., *A Religion for One World*
Scott, Clinton Lee, *Some Things Remembered*
Scott, Clinton Lee, *The Universalist Church of America, a Short History*

Chapter 7

Patton Rites:
Fond Memories of Patton's Place
at Charles and Mt. Vernon

Charles A. Reinhardt

You read, "One may set his hand to the task of building a new kind of church adapted to the new age, thus creating a demonstration center that will prove what can be done by a radical reconstruction." Indeed! Those words of Clarence Skinner, from a sermon published in his 1931 book *A Free Pulpit in Action*, express in a calm, deliberate way what was happening in the Charles Street Meeting House in Boston midway through the twentieth century.

What got underway in 1949 in that newly Universalist Meeting House with Kenneth Patton as the newly called minister was deliberate, all right, but the action in the formerly Black Baptist church on the corner of Charles and Mt. Vernon Streets was anything but calm. That is, it was anything but calm or dignified in Clarence Skinner's Victorian gentlemanly style. The Charles Street Meeting House project had sprung out of the articulate conversations of Clinton and Mary Scott. Clint headed up the Massachusetts Universalist Convention. Clint, his wife Mary, and their son Peter played important roles in the new congregation taking shape.

In conversations with the Scotts in the summer of 1949 I learned how pleased they were that Patton had accepted the invitation to that new leadership post. He was clearly the energetic, if somewhat diamond-in-the-rough, articulate poetic type, a leader of great promise who had just given up his pulpit in the Unitarian church of Madison, Wisconsin. The Scotts and others viewed him as one of the most-likely-to-succeed liberal Unitarian or Universalist ministers around in those days. Patton was from upland corn prairie, a Midwesterner who was noisily impatient with what he considered the lazy, self-satisfied ways of the two Boston-based bastions of liberal churchmanship, the American Unitarian Association and the Univeralist Church of America. In just a short time the Meeting House became something like a boisterous speakeasy of the soul, rude and ready with unchurchmanly arguments favored by Ken. He relished knowing that the continental headquarters of both the Universalists and Unitarians were only a few blocks away on Beacon Hill. Like the flinty barkeeps within the shadows of Boston churches, Patton was delighted to be so close to concentrations of public emotion. Three distinguished Unitarian churches, King's Chapel, Arlington Street Church, and the First Church of Boston, were also short walks or cab rides away. Suddenly there was a unique quartet of liberal congregations in a tight urban setting.

For Ken, proximity meant power, as he gloatingly admitted. Fate had landed him in "The Hub" where all eyes would be on him and his congregation as they built "a new kind of church adapted to the new age, thus creating a demonstration center that will prove what can be done by a radical reconstruction." His attitude was a pure dare to anyone in a hierarchy to stop him. A prophet had arrived in Boston.

Ken Patton was a self-styled prophet in the grand Biblical style. He proclaimed doom, by god! Well, not by God, because he was careful to point out that his position was theologically far enough left for him to speak in the name of scientific humanism. He told me that the first time I entered his office in the church undercroft. Ken made clear that there was no room in his thinking for one god or many. Unless, of course, you were discussing historical facts. Theology was out and historicity and anthropology were in. It was to be just the facts, man, nothing but the facts, please, when discussing reports of the holy presence with this prophet. I stood there, wondering what to do with my pantheistic Emersonian transcendentalism. Ken's mysticism went as far as Walt Whitman's *Leaves of Grass*, the family of man, and all scientifically observable star stuff. His scientific humanism had its points. But did it have to be so certain and self-satsified? Was humanistic, mystical atheism the only way for the modern free mind to go? Did the liturgies of churches need to be cleansed of all the old spiritual poetics? This prophet in the center of things, Boston, the Hub, was sure that the time had arrived to cleanse the temple.

Leaving Methodist connections and four years of experience as a student minister, I was headed for graduate work at Harvard Divinity School and, hopefully, a career in the "liberal ministry." Tolerant as Protestantism could be at midcentury, the natural limits of Methodist tolerance were quite familiar to me. The liberal openness on spiritual matters advertised so well in Unitarian and Universalist circles appealed to me. Emersonian pantheistic musings as well as an Alfred North Whitehead kind of evolutionary god-in-process concept looked good to me. But abruptly, Ken Patton confronted me with a phalanx of arguments about the absurdity of superstitious speculations dressed in the latest, or almost the latest, literary styles. Doom was around the corner for the human family if we religious leaders allowed superstitious nonsense to go on much longer! Ken's facial muscles were taut as he spoke. His arms and hands chopped the air. Whoopee, I thought, Patton's hot as a pistol. Protestants, Catholics, and religious liberals alike, all of them, were headed for absurdity and oblivion unless they cleansed themselves of old beliefs and appealed rationally and truthfully to a brighter, better educated public. Ah, this was real fire-in-the-belly stuff.

My first encounter with Patton was one August Sunday in 1950 in the old Universalist church in Gloucester. Finding out only later that Clarence Skinner had just died in that same summer season, I think back now on that morning in church listening to Patton, the guest minister newly arrived in the Boston area, I later realized he had grabbed the torch of a new Universalism as it left Skinner's hand. The hot homiletical point that cool morning in the antique air of Gloucester's Universalist meeting house had everything to do with, in Skinner's words, "building a new kind of church adapted to the new age, thus creating a demonstration center that will prove what can be done by a radical reconstruction."

The sermon sounded like a new kind of preacher's hell-fire. Ken's long preface to the positive point of the sermon proclaimed doom. The Universalist church, he said firmly, "has gone to seed." The end is near. Universalism is going under, and the Unitarians are next, you can be sure. His friend, Clint Scott of the Universalist State Convention, had provided Ken with a gloomy box score: one Massachusetts Universalist church had disappeared in each of the preceding fifty years. Referring to that, Ken adopted the solemn tone of the famous newscaster Edward R. Murrow, he of the voice of cultivated gloom. "We are now close to the end," he said.

Yet, there is a bright side, he said, however elusive that may have been to the aging crowd in church that morning. What we can look forward to, he said very assuredly, is a new beginning. From a plant gone to seed a new beginning is possible. Now we have a natural new beginning in the offing if we do something about it.

But to me it was noticeable that the tone of homiletic hope showed possible inner conflict in the preacher. Jonah-like, would this man continue to want punishment for the folks he would convert? For himself, too? Perhaps his sermons over the years were the clearest expression of some fierce inner battles. Although I kept busy with my own work in churches, this ecstatic prophet held my attention over the next couple of decades. During that time he moved from Boston to Ridgewood, New Jersey, and the better-established Unitarian congregation there.

Serious as the Corn Belt Protestant of his first inspirations, Ken ran with the flaming torch of reform throughout his career. This man was offended by what he believed to be unfortunate compromises characterized by the preaching from various pulpits, liberal and conservative. Not long after he had established himself as Boston's most outspoken prophet of the Eisenhower era, he took on the preachers in a sermon: "The Prostitution of the Clergy." It was a clarion call to uncharacteristic candor in church. He charged that ministers and priests were guilty of gussying up their messages to please the tastes and prejudices of those sitting comfortably in the pews. It was the way prostitutes on the street went about their work. It was shamefully commercial and immoral, he bellowed.

In the aftermath of that one the Rev. Mr. Patton braved a storm of reaction. Still, as interesting as it was to hear the clerical outrage around Boston, it was Ken's mixture of pleasure and guilt that caught my attention. I had gone into his office one morning on my way into a meeting at Universalist headquarters up on Beacon Street. I could see right away that Ken was on the edge of hysteria. On the one hand he relished the impact of what he had said in the sermon—or in the title itself. "The Prostitution of the Clergy" had (he was sure) dealt a blow to religious styles that had outlived their legitimacy. On the other hand, he had blown the whistle on brothers of the cloth. He alternated between chortles and righteous little defenses. He looked like a kid who had just tattled on others in the classroom. I decided that perhaps all the prophets, at least from Amos onward, had been tortured by inner doubts, especially when they believed that they were both right and heard. Such is the curse of righteousness, right or wrong.

It was a notorious Easter sermon in Ken's early years in Boston that got under the skin of laity and clergy alike. Again, the title was a grabber: "Upsadaisy." Ken had run across a *New Yorker* a cartoon that showed a little girl sprawled on the sidewalk, having tumbled from her stroller. The toddler was looking up at her nanny saying, "Upsadaisy hell, that hurt." The clear intent of the sermon was to point out that the usual Easter message from pulpits all over was to gloss over the real pain of Jesus having been executed. No amount of posthumous theologizing about God's reputed plan for death and resurrection could comfort a sensitive mind. Upsadaisy hell, said the angry Patton, himself a former Disciples of Christ minister. That unfortunately ignorant crowd of Romans and Judeans had wrongly crucified a thoroughly decent and promising young man. Perhaps identifying strongly with Jesus, Ken appeared seriously moved as he discussed that sermon with a few of us one day. He was appalled that others were accusing him of being impious and cynically flip. He said if the critics had actually read what was in the printed sermon itself they would know that only the sermon's title and the cartoon itself were funny, and that was dark humor in any case. Serious stuff, in other words.

Ken was worked up. His prophetic fire on the matter had not cooled even many weeks following the general brouhaha in liberal church circles. Because I was in the neighborhood of the Charles Street Meeting House at least once a month, I had the habit of dropping by to see what he was up to. Rather early on there, Ken was hard at work on the sights and sounds of the sanctuary space as they were being adapted for his Sunday services. Over the years he created a whole series of religious symbols that would be on display at all times. It was the usual collection, of course: the Cross, the star of David, yin yang, the crescent of Muhammad. As time went on he added the symbols of ancient and primitive groups, and even one for capitalists, the dollar sign. All of them were clearly recognizable from anywhere in the sanctuary.

Also early on, Ken, probably alone without help from church members, put together for display a collection of major anthropological, mystical, theological, scriptural and philosophical books bearing on religious experience. A large, long and low bookcase was installed to "showcase" the books, and it was nicely visible within the elegant Greek proscenium. He thought an illuminated globe should be on top of the bookcase, and by and by, it too appeared. As if all of that was not enough symbolism, two other visuals graced the proscenium platform. Because Patton the preacher needed a better pulpit that would fit the general scheme, a modern, Bauhaus-simple design came about, with a large sound system inside for recorded music. It had a black facing that became the backdrop for one or another of the brass symbols suitable for any given service theme. Enough already, some folks said. Still, Ken continued to argue for two more symbols. Two of monumental size.

I caught Ken on his hands and knees one day, down in the church basement. He flinched when teased about possibly praying. Quickly recovering some humor, he proudly showed me the first of a number of panels he was painting. He looked like a happy kid building a terrific model airplane. When completed, the panels would show stars against a dark blue background and would fill the entire wall of the sanctuary proscenium. The spiral nebula in Andromeda would, he said, remind the congregation of the vital relationship between humankind and the vast natural setting in which life and intelligent, questing awareness have taken place. "This," he said, "is the stuff of wonder and humility."

Questioning Ken about these bold moves of his, and occasionally arguing with him, as a number of us from Harvard Divinity School did, was great fun. If pressed hard enough, he, with a ready smirk and eyes dancing, would drop what he was doing and take us into his office. There, he would grab a volume of some kind off the shelf (and there were lots of shelves and lots of books), and he would quote chapter and verse of some author's work. One of his favorites was Eustace Hayden of the University of Chicago, the noted academic who had supplied Ken with many of his ideas about a rational, appreciative approach to religion and ancient secular wisdom. Science too, as a key, was of utmost significance as it impinged on our thinking about anything and everything. As a young preacher deeply moved by Hayden's hard-edged teaching, Ken was hungry for hard facts of history and the human psyche as they informed the ultimate questions of mortality and morality. Hallmark greeting card-sentiments about religion were not for this guy.

Stephen Spender dealt with the subject of scientific objectivity when he took a close look at Goethe. He mentioned the term "faith-determined poetic mind" as a fitting one for the great eighteenth-century mind, and wrote, "To study facts and draw whatever conclusions led from them, to look too scientifically into the unknown, to question skeptically the mysterious, was as blasphemous to him as to his very different contemporary William Blake." But Ken said repeatedly and in his own way, that we, like himself, should be glad to study facts, draw whatever conclusions led from them, look as scientifically as we could into the unknown, and question skeptically the mysterious. A favorite quotation of his from Thoreau was, "I want to cut a broad swath and shave close, to drive life into a corner, and reduce it to its lowest terms. If it proves to be mean, then to get the whole and genuine meanness of it, and publish its meanness to the world; or if it is sublime, to know it by experience, and to be able to give a true account of it." As a member of the 1960s hymnbook commission, Ken saw to it that those hard edged-words got into the *Hymns for the Celebration of Life*.

For him, to do other than "drive life into a corner" was blasphemous. Although he had high regard for Goethe and Blake, mentioning them from time to time, they were obviously of the eighteenth century, and he had fashioned his own poetic mind as a twentieth-century mind as he studied at the feet of great University of Chicago intellects. To be sure, and in keeping with what science was telling us about about our bodies and intellects, Ken in his "faith-determined" manner referred to our human condition as mind-body. He would not, could not, separate the spirit from the flesh. It was there in the natural combination he found the mysterious connections with the rest of the cosmos. For him, the more facts the better, no matter how much they seemed to be in conflict. Ken made it clear in his arguments with us down in that book-lined office of his that it required the poetic, religious mind to deal effectively with the random chaos, synergy, and intricately connected potential of the universe. He was delighted, visibly delighted to be a "Universalist" free of the old parochial faiths of Christianity. Facts and more facts mixed in with a Whitmanesque love of life that had become his faith. He claimed to have no fear of looking "too scientifically into the unknown," backing life into a corner and finding out whether it proved to be mean or sublime. Or both.

So the work for this man who would "set his hand to the task of building a new kind of church adapted to the new age, thus creating a demonstration center that will prove what can be done by a radical reconstruction" went forward with much arguing and often defensive energy. While his congregation remained quite small, a few enchanted fans (or followers) showed up from surrounding Universalist and Unitarian churches. My congregation in nearby Saugus had active members who were drawn to Patton's efforts, most notably the Sawyer family, three of whom would eventually do graduate studies in religion at Harvard and Starr King School for the Ministry in Berkeley, and two of those would become ordained ministers (Alan and Paul Sawyer). And largely because of the combined efforts of Clinton Scott and Ken, and the political difficulties in which they found themselves in official Universalist circles, Alan Sawyer Sr. ran for and won the office of President of the Universalist Church of America.

In those years Ken was a lightning rod for trouble in liberal church politics. Avowed Universalist Christians charged that Patton was leading church newcomers to abandon Jesus and his heavenly father. Then there were the Unitarian and Universalist liberals who were already in trouble in their congregations. Their "secular" interests bothered old-line conservatives in some of the well-established churches. Evolution, economic and racial justice, humanistic ethics in public policy, progressive education, psychiatry, and international affairs were the hot topics that Patton and his friends were calling the growing edge. Then a few of us with Ken's help created a little journal with the actual name *The Edge*.

Many a pulpit in the mid-twentieth century got on controversial topics regularly and many a liberal minister in New England worried that Patton's radically different moves would destabilize things. After all, it was the age of McCarthyism and the John Birch Society. Liberals were suspected of atheistic communist sympathies. And along came Ken Patton! At the annual meetings of both liberal denominations, colleagues would argue heatedly with him and talk about him behind his back. While at the continental level there were few political moves to clip Ken's wings, the Massachusetts State Convention of Universalists became the scene of many a pitched battle to end convention support (financial) for the Meeting House and, not incidentally, Ken himself. There was also the effort to discourage the interest of young, about-to-be-ordained ministers. I seem to remember Ken complaining that like Socrates, he was being charged with the corruption of youth. I know of at least one candidate for ministry who was asked, "Young man, what is your stand on Ken Patton?"

Of course Ken loved it, or at least said he did. He said he measured his success by the flak that was coming down. Another time when I found him on his knees he was upstairs in the sanctuary. My question about his prayer life was answered with a sharp remark about the stick-in-the-muds of ministry who feared to do new things they should be doing. What he was doing at the moment was laying a new linoleum floor in the middle of what had been done to create a church in the round. Pews were set in the now familiar circles around a colorful new floor displaying a polar projection of the globe. I'm not sure that a full congregation would get much of a view of that world motif in the center of the floor. Maybe people sitting behind those front rows would remember what they saw when they had first walked into the sanctuary for the morning service. In any event, Ken was sure that it was a necessary step in reconstructing the church and its symbolism in the "new age." By the time the "global projection" went down on the floor, the brass symbols of the world's religions had been moved from the columns of the proscenium to the panels around the balconies.

What I remember next is the printing press. For any of us ministers in the small-church game, the mimeograph machine and its diet of smelly black ink and wood-pulp paper was a serious, not easily-to-be-dismissed tool of the trade. Ken was eager to put his "faith-determined poetic" output of sermons, responsive readings, meditative poetry, and new hymn lyrics into print. Therefore, the accursed but manageably inexpensive mimeograph process had been the way to go for him. He had a lot to say. Lots. On any Sunday you would find the literature table in the church foyer loaded with his output, new items showing up regularly. But the sulfide pulp mimeo paper was a crumby way to appear in print and he knew it.

I was not surprised when I dropped by one day to find a huge, old-fashioned printing press sitting on the side of the big meeting room in the church basement. Ken emerged from his office, a serious look on his face. He looked like a museum official about to unveil a significant new acquisition of sculpture. Before long, he was smiling like a kid with a new slingshot. In those old days of the midtwentieth century one could always tell if a clergyman was doing his own mimeographing because there would be ink stains on his hands and under the fingernails. However, once he had the printing press to play with, the new ink stains on his hands made mimeo stains look minor. Now, Ken looked like someone who had been working under the hood of an old car. But, God knows (forgive me, Ken), once the printing press began its clanking work, he was soaring at new altitudes.

Out of that period came a great proliferation of new hymns, readings, even books. As Unitarians and Universalists of the 1960s and 1970s know, the name of Kenneth Patton appears again and again in the *Hymns for the Celebration of Life,* which was published in the mid-Sixties. Perhaps Ken would have made major contributions to that hymnbook in any case. But I think that it was that big black clanking printing press that helped him get into high gear. For clearing out the tangled underbrush of sentimental Christian liturgical notions that came out of the previous nineteen centuries, the pen was mightier than the sword, and the poetic Patton-run printing press was stealthier and more effective than the wars between royal and churchly European powers and later, the crude tactics of Marxist states. Page by page, that oily, inky press thunking away under Ken's hand in the church basement was doing a major part of the "radical reconstruction" of the church long hoped for by the liberals of the free church.

The ideas of Ralph Waldo Emerson, Olympia Brown, Theodore Parker, Clarence Skinner, and Norbert Capek come to mind. The list is long. There were many outspoken reform-minded women as well as men in Unitarian and Universalist pulpits across the continent during almost two centuries of American history. Still, none of them appears to have had the immediate impact on the Sunday service that did Patton once that press of his got into action. Even without the speed of offset presses, let alone the Internet with its e-mail and chat rooms, Ken's printed words of "radical reconstruction" replaced much of what was familiar to church-goers' eyes and ears. The mystical, ebullient naturalism of Walt Whitman's *Leaves of Grass* with the latest twentieth-century discoveries of neurological and psychological sciences thrown in became the reference material and language that all but replaced the familiar pieties of even the most liberal Protestant liturgies. The idealism nowadays attributed to flower children—fair-minded images of a happier society with collegial acceptance of one another—replaced solemn confessional prayers and readings that had been the language of worship for a long time.

The reference to flower children aside, Ken Patton was not all smiles and sunshine. He wasn't into hugs. What I discovered early on in my friendship with him was that he was a stern moralist. With cutting remarks about his critics he was an aggressive prophet, a prophet of the old school, proclaiming doom about one and another kind of societal injustice. His sermons often touched on America's addiction to the military-industrial complex. I gave Ken a ride somewhere in Boston one day. I was driving my plain but still-and-all, very shiny new two door-Ford. He owned a well-worn old car at the time. So he sang to me, "Oh you can't get to heaven, in a brand new Ford. . . ." He didn't like it. Not one bit. Tough, I thought to myself, and yet I did feel some guilt about it. His moral judgment had stirred some familiar Methodist guilt deep in my gut.

The prophetic angle of his preaching often appealed to the citizen in us to force our nation and the expanding global civilization to eliminate poverty, racism, ethnic rivalry, and warfare. He railed against the competitive ostentations and power plays that trash the human family. And so he made remarks condemning even liberals who profited from the avaricious economy that had come about in post World War II period. Around the time he preached my ordination sermon in 1952, I mentioned to him the two churches that I was considering for the next step in my career. The first was a rural Universalist congregation in the South. He got a sour look on his face, said, "Have a Coke!," and then adding something about the underlying lynch-mob mentality of people who go along with racial segregation. The fact that I was considering a member congregation of the Universalist Church of America cut no ice in the ensuing argument with him. The Universalists "down there" were false liberals in his eyes because they were such a part of the "below the Mason-Dixon Line" culture.

The other congregation I mentioned in that conversation was in the Boston suburbs. It too fell short because in his eyes the people there were quite successful in the unjust postwar economy. I had known that Ken carried his moral criticism into the very heart of everyday dealings with those around him, but what I wanted was a less emotionally slanted and cursory opinion from a colleague who had observed more liberal churches that I had. Perhaps puritanical in a way fitting for a new age, Ken was religiously consistent to his prophetic muse. A prominent Unitarian minister who had tangled with Ken at several conferences told me after one bruising encounter that Ken was not the kind of colleague one could argue with at meetings and then go off to dinner with and enjoy a drink and good steak: "He's an angry man, a very angry man."

Rough as Ken could be on his colleagues, he was even harder on himself. He appeared to fear success of any kind. As much as he relished acclaim, he also distrusted it. Our good friends Clint and Mary Scott wanted him to be successful at building the Meeting House as the church of their dreams. It was why he was their top choice for that new pulpit in

Boston, the Hub. Believing that his very effective sermons would attract many good people, the Scotts had had visions of a resurgence of the kind of public enthusiasm for liberal religion that had greeted Theodore Parker in Boston and Thomas Starr King in San Francisco a century before. But, as it soon became apparent, Ken was not successful at building a strong congregation and it probably meant that he felt a stab of guilt whenever he thought about the Scotts. I never heard Ken say anything good or bad about them. Nor did I hear the Scotts say much about Ken. Silence from them had become the norm as Ken began to belittle the whole idea of success in building a congregation. Oddly, his sermons appeared to me to become even better, more powerful and incisive as time went by. And the Scotts, not just out of loyalty but with genuine respect for Ken's sermons, were in the congregation most Sundays.

When the new hymnal appeared in 1964, Ken's name appeared so many times in credits for hymns, meditations, and responsive readings that some people referred to it as the Ken Patton hymnal. That embarrassed him too, though years later when receiving the distinguished service award from the UUA, he said, "It's about time; why have you waited so long?" He smiled and waited for the crowd to react. He looked happy at the chance to ham it up.

He had served prominently as a member of the Hymnbook Commission in the Sixties. It worried him that the new hymnal was weighted with so much of his own work, not only because of the inevitable criticism that would be directed his way but also because if any other colleague had had as much successful influence, he for one would have been critical. As much as Ken liked to show off his poetic talent, a prophetic gloom was always there to get in the way of the satisfaction he might have felt. He was addicted to proclaiming doom on the one hand and to waxing poetic about the happy, affectionate human family on the other. Exalted dreams of happiness did not rest comfortably with that kind of critical mind. He and his wife Betty came to dinner at my home one night shortly after my wife Carol and I became parents for the first time. After some easy conversation we invited them in to see three-month-old Hans, who was asleep in the other room. Betty was elated; Ken remained fixed in his chair. He turned to me and said, "I'll take a look at him when he's grown up, when we can have an intelligent conversation." Intelligent conversation to Ken was an exchange of real ideas. Life is too short to waste on mere pleasantries, he had said about casual conversations. That was over a cup of coffee somewhere, I no longer remember where. But the intensity was unforgettable.

As I look back there is a question that lingers: Did Ken Patton have a hard time shuttling back and forth between the poles of his poetic muse, between happy "human togetherness!" (his phrase) and his prophetic edge? To him, working and living on the "edge" had profound meaning, as his choice of "The Edge" as the title of the journal we published would suggest. I think he spent a lot of time in that confusing in-between territory, one moment enchanted by visions of great beauty, the next moment tortured by realistic observations of hell in everyday life. One of his early Charles Street sermons, prophetic to the core, painted the picture of modern warfare's "flaming jellies" that in fact were to be used in Vietnam only a few years from then.

Stupidity, avarice and violence were never far from his thinking. But neither were the warmth of lovers and parents, the affection of companions, and the genius of artists. Never to remain enchanted for very long, nor defeated by his own prophecies of doom, he went back and forth, always in some kind of pain, it seemed. His critical comments regarding others were always from the doom side of the equation; his occasional bursts of ecstasy about the friends and artists he admired came when he was close to his enchanted muse. Yet I rarely heard him speak well of others—colleagues, for instance. He did mention Vincent Silliman a number of times, and Arthur Foote, two members of the 1964 Hymnbook Commission. And he was enthusiastic about the sermons of Jesse Cavalier, but that was about it. I think he kept quiet about the rest of us because we, like he himself, were flawed and unable to perform as he expected. Perhaps he often seemed agitated when he saw many of us colleagues because on that interior map of his we appeared somewhere between the poles of beautiful enchantment and gloomy realism.

In one of my last conversations with Ken he told me that he wanted to spend his final years studying art. He was living not far from New York when he retired and he felt drawn to the museums, galleries, and libraries where he could immerse himself in the works of the truly great creators. For him as for Hippocrates, life is short and art long. Why waste time repeating the dull and outrageous mistakes of the past? I believe he really did think that life could be so very beautiful, that we could learn to connect in loving good ways. As he said, "The church of tomorrow . . . will make honest and whole the cravings and appetites . . . leading to the joys of fullness and self realization . . . uniting us with our companions of the journey, helping us in our pilgrimage along the road between the cities of birth and death." For me he was a tonic that got the second half of the twentieth century off to an amazing start.

For the liberal religious movement now called Unitarian Universalism, Ken Patton created worship material that became a rite of passage. The liberal churches of the second half of the twentieth century perhaps represent what is in the long view a still-young faith. His sermons for those of us lucky enough to have heard them were what we might think of now as a fringe benefit. And yet, those prophetic ideas that were developed in sermonic form, so biting and gloomy at times, stimulated his soaring poetic flights. His sermon ideas stimulated his poetry and generated a large field of energy for "a new kind of church adapted to the new age." For a politicized nation with a very spotty record of concern for education and basic human welfare, Ken Patton's ecstatic visions are quite a tonic. As the twenty-first century begins it is interesting to think of his words that could inform ordinary folks all over:

> We will make a world for the gladness of children, bringing to them the conviction of their worth and beauty which their beings crave.

> We will gather a store of love for youth, troubled in the rising turbulence of life, to guide them into maturity with less of loneliness and torture.

> We will find useful tasks for their hands, that they may learn to create with clean joy.

We will gather a store of love for parents, for if the homes of the land are stark and brutal, then are we indeed poor.

Our chief labor is the building of homes, and our knowledge will be increased to set the seasons of childhood and parenthood in the ways of goodness.

We will gather a store of love for the aged, whose days have been wrung with our follies and hurts. Our land will be a large home for the elders. . . .

We will turn our whole persons to the use of love and understanding.

Chapter 8

Personal Experiences
at the Charles Street Meeting House

Charlotte Sawyer Fish

My first introduction to the Charles Street Meeting House was as a high school student. During spring break from the Northfield School, I sat in Chuck Reinhardt's living room in Saugus, Massachusetts. There were long discussions about life, religion and politics with Hugh Weston, Chuck, Clint Scott, Horton Colbert and my dad, Alan Sawyer. The Meeting House was often discussed. There was much talk about the Charles Street Meeting House as a center of the "new" Universalism.

Universalism was not a new idea in my family. My grandmother was the daughter of Adam Winslow, who donated land in Cumberland, Maine, to build a Universalist church there. My grandmother belonged to First Parish Universalist, in Saugus, Massachusetts where Charles Reinhardt was the new young minister. Chuck was encouraged to come east from Minnesota to study at Harvard by Clinton Lee Scott. Many other young liberal ministers who were part of this "new blood" were encouraged to come to the Massachusetts area by Scott. The Meeting House was the center of the world-universe-embracing Universalism that was an extension of the foundation of ideas that had been historically Universalism.

On a Sunday morning during that spring break I walked though the doors of the Meeting House and felt an immediate and strong connection to the large mural of the universe painted on the wall at the front of the church. Music from another culture was surrounding me. Brass symbols of world religions hung on either side of the mural. Art objects of other religions were placed carefully around the space as part of the service. Loose-leaved notebooks filled with the morning's hymns and readings had been thoughtfully composed for us to use. I had never experienced any service so open, so world-oriented. Kenneth Patton gave his sermon; many readings were written by him or came from other cultures. I was completely overcome with a sense of belonging to our diverse world culture—truly universal.

Our whole family stood up to become members of the First Universalist Church in Saugus shortly after that. I and my grandfather, Frederick Sawyer, mother, Ruth, father Alan, and two brothers, Alan Jr. and Paul, all became members on the same morning. We lived in Saugus, and my parents taught Sunday School there. However, we continued our interest in the Meeting House. Boston was a little far for active membership.

During my later teen years, while I was away at school and college, my dad and mother were involved with Universalist activities. My dad, a lawyer, was President of the Universalist Church of America and was crucially involved at the Andover meetings when the Charles Street Meeting House was "saved" as the experimental church supported by the UCA. His experience and knowledge as a lawyer were needed to help the group of ministers and lay people who fought to keep this liberal center alive and central to the movement.

Several years later, in 1959, I returned to Massachusetts as a young single mother with two preschool children. Again, I decided to attend the Charles Street Meeting House, where I met Joseph Fish. Joe was a young physicist who was a friend of Ralph Edlund and his sister, Charlotte. They had been a second family to him while he was growing up with Ralph's son, Robert. They were old Universalists in Dorchester, Massachusetts, and influenced Joe a great deal. They were among the backbone of workers at the Charles Street Meeting House; they were jewelry makers by hobby and became involved in designing and crafting the wonderful brass symbols which were used at the Meeting House and are now at Starr King School of the Ministry in California. Joe helped to bring the old Green estate organ—in shopping bags—to Charles Street, and was in charge of rebuilding the organ, not just on Friday night work nights, but at other times as well.

In 1959 Joe and I were married at the church picnic at Marie Lyon's house in Newton. We then moved to Concord, about 30 miles west of Boston, and commuted to Charles Street for Friday night work night and Sunday programs. Joe was on the board; he played the piano, and after the organ was rebuilt, played the organ for years. He donated countless hours to help the church. We both sang in the a capella choir of four to six voices. Friday nights were spent putting together the open hymnals for the Sunday service, choir practice, making and polishing brass symbols, cleaning the church, talking, and working on the organ and art collection. Roland Hueston, Marie Lyons, Ralph and Charlotte Edlund, Viola Pease, Mary Lillie, Una Ford, Ruth and Charles Vickery, and Charle McCormack are all names and faces that come to mind. I was director of religious education and a board member for many years; as a trained teacher, I helped as much as possible. We had a small, ever-changing group and it was a difficult task. The most exciting part of the program was participating in the spring, fall, and winter festivals—especially the dance portions with Diane and Al Pesso. We also made an arrangement with Arlington St. (Unitarian) Church to have the older children attend Sunday school there at one point. We encouraged the children to attend Ferry Beach camps also.

Charles Street was always at the center of liberal activities in Boston. During the Sixties, we were always willing to be open for all groups; the African-American Museum kept its collections and meetings there until they acquired their own space in the neighborhood. Stokely Carmichel (later Kwame Ture) was hidden (from the FBI, I think) one Sunday morning in our Sunday school room; all types of anti-war, Black activist, political groups and later women's rights, feminist, and gay and lesbian groups used our building. Often we were an embarrassment to the UUA and conservative Beacon Hill groups at that time.

Kenneth Patton was not an easy person. He had difficulty working cooperatively with the people in the church. He was often dictatorial in his methods. My mother said, "He loves Humanity, but has difficulty with most humans." When my youngest of four children was about to be born, I spent the Sunday morning singing in the choir, mopping the child care room, and helping with the monthly dinner. As we arrived home in Concord, I realized I had better drive to the hospital. My son Karl was born shortly after. Kenneth was concerned with whether I would be there the next Sunday to sing for the Spring Festival. (I was!) He had asked me a few weeks before, "When IS that baby going to be born, anyway?!" He was "short" with people and hurt their feelings many times. But we were all forgiving and loyal because we all believed that the work we were part of was so important.

Kenneth left the Meeting House after he remarried and had another child. Our group could not support his family with what we were able to provide. For years we kept the Meeting House open and continued much of the work Kenneth Patton had started. Alan and Carl Seaburg and Randall Gibson gave a great deal to the group with little support from the UUA. We had many monetary problems with the building. Slates fell from the roof to the street; maintenance was not kept up. UUA headquarters was pressuring us to close the building and consolidate with Arlington Street Church. Dana Greeley, then a minister in Concord, arrived at my house in Concord on Sunday afternoon to see "how the poor Meeting House is doing" and tried to get Joe and me, as Board members of Charles Street, to close it down. His wife, Debbie Greeley, also approached me about consolidation with Arlington Street. The gay rights work established by Randall Gibson was embarrassing to the UUA headquarters at that time. Money that had been given for special programs was taken back, leaving us in a more difficult financial position.

In 1978 I moved to the U.S. Virgin Islands and was no longer able to be part of the struggle to keep Charles Street Meeting House together. There was no support from Beacon Street (UUA headquarters) and the struggle was too late and too little to keep this center alive. The building is now part of the gentrified boutique-antique area of Beacon Hill.

Interior of the Meeting House

Photo: *The Universalist Publishing House*, Records, 1862–1961, Andover Harvard Theological Library of Harvard Divinity School, Cambridge, Massachusetts.

Chapter 9

Meeting House Days, 1962–1968

Alan Seaburg

It was a sunny, if coldish, Sunday morning and we were walking down Charles Street (the traffic pattern then was from Beacon Street to the Mass General Hospital complex) to attend the 11 A.M. service at the Charles Street Meeting House, or as it was more popularly termed by us regulars, the Meeting House (MH). The "we" were Jean and Alan Seaburg, our two daughters Carolyn and Ann, and my brother, Carl Seaburg. I had just parked the car in the garage under Boston Common, for we were all living then in Medford and so had to drive into Boston for MH services and activities.

As we headed down Charles we passed three taxis at the curb, all with their driver's doors open, all with their radios blasting. The news was electrifying: Jack Ruby had just shot and killed Lee Harvey Oswald. We stopped and listened for a moment, and then continued walking to the Meeting House. The meetings of that tiny but wonderful congregation, operating in its inadequate red-brick 1807 Asher Benjamin building, and with its determined but often acrimonious minister, Ken Patton, was always far more intellectually exciting and emotionally satisfying than almost any event the media felt fit to report on during that brilliant, eventful decade in America, the 1960s.

During the period 1962–1968 I knew the Meeting House from three perspectives: as a member of its congregation, as chair of its board of trustees, and as co-minister with Ken after he had accepted the position of minister of the Unitarian Society of Ridgewood, New Jersey.

The first two roles are happily blended together in my memory; and while the third is more distinct, it resembled the others, for during the three years that I served the Meeting House as its co-minister (1965–1968) we followed much the same impulses and program opportunities that had come to characterize the institution, except for the activities of its press which Ken had largely transferred from Boston to Ridgewood. [See my address on "Worship" which was published in *Unity* in 1965 and Conrad Wright's reference to it in his book, *Walking Together*.] Also, the basic Patton congregation remained intact during this period. It did not disperse, for the most part, until the mid-1970s. The only major change was that I was now responsible for supervising the Sunday services, preaching once a month, looking after the building and the activities that took place there, and serving as "host" for the Meeting House family. Ken, of course, continued to inspire the Meeting House vision and remained in charge of the Friday evening services, which he came up weekly to conduct.

Before he moved to Ridgewood Ken had stopped in to visit Dana McLean Greeley, the President of the UUA, to share with him his "dreams" for both societies. After that visit Greeley wrote Patton: "I think it is fair for me to say that we do believe that you are undertaking a very difficult task, or two difficult tasks, in endeavoring to serve both the Ridgewood Church as its full time minister and the Charles Street Meeting House with no less loyalty than you have given to it over the last fifteen years." Greeley went on to wish him well but, of course, his concern was on the mark. As for Ken, he was to write to Ray Hopkins at the UUA almost two years later that his "own commitment to the Meeting House is continuous."(1)

To fully appreciate the inner spirit that defined membership and involvement for the small core group that made it possible for Patton and his congregation to nurture the Meeting House experiment, it is necessary to know how it utilized the space available to it in the old nineteenth-century-designed building which the Massachusetts Universalist Convention (MUC) had purchased for it to develop within. Just as that local convention, and its parent group the Universalist Church of America, and then the Unitarian Universalist Association, never provided adequate financial support (outside of building maintenance) for this religious experiment, which many in that association now like to boast about, (2) it also stuck the Meeting House with a structure costly to run and whose space—and there is no better word than this—sucked. Even if Patton called it in 1949 a "lovely old building," one needs to remember that lovely old buildings do not necessarily make for good space for religious endeavors.

The building had just two floors arranged in the familiar way: an upstairs auditorium for worship and a lower floor for all other activities. In his book, *A Religion for One World: Art and Symbols for a Universal Religion*, Ken fully described the sanctuary. But in many ways, the floor below was just as vital to the workability of the Meeting House experiment.

When you entered the main entrance of the building, you found a small lobby, with two rounding staircases to the upper floor, and with a few steps between them leading down through a short hallway to the first floor. In the hallway, on the right were steps leading down to the public rest rooms; on the left a door led to a series of private rooms. (3) Several years after the MH was launched, the MUC moved its headquarters from 16 Beacon Street to this area. Indeed, the room where I met the MUC Fellowship Committee to be examined for the fitness of my entering the ministry, later became the bedroom of my two young daughters. After the merger in 1961 of the Universalist and Unitarian parent groups, which resulted in the MUC being absorbed in 1962 by the Unitarian Universalist Association, the private rooms became the living quarters for Ken, his second wife, Mitzi, and their first child, Dag. (4) When Patton left for New Jersey, my family and I occupied them, and when we left, Randy Gibson did.(5)

All of the space described so far took up about half of the available area on that first floor. The rest was divided as follows: a boiler room, which once also housed the MH press; Ken's office which contained a bunk bed where he slept when he came up from New Jersey to conduct the Friday evening service; and on the Charles Street side, a kitchen, and a work room where we prepared on Friday nights (the weekly work night although for a while after Ken went to NJ it was moved to Thursday night because of the Friday service) the Sunday open hymnal booklets; did press work such as gathering, folding, and collating of its various publications; and did custodial tasks, etc. Then there was a hallway to Charles Street and a room for the children that was later used by the American Museum of Negro History for its displays. The remaining space was a general all-purpose hall, where after the service on Sunday we met to discuss the address, have coffee, tea, snacks, and once a month the Sunday dinners. Along its walls were hung many of the Kaethe Kollwitz lithographs and etchings that Ken had gathered as well as other art illustrating the religions of the world.

The lower floor became more crowded when the Meeting House, in 1965, in an effort to fund its budget, began to rent the hall during the week to nearby Emerson College which used it for its dance department.(6) Emerson also rented the main auditorium weekly for its large lecture classes, not possessing at this time adequate space elsewhere. To fully utilize the space, Emerson, with the agreement of the MH, removed all the pews and purchased folding pink chairs (they became the property of the MH) which could be arranged in rows for their classes (7) and in a circle for the MH on Sundays. This, of course, involved lots of extra work, and when the floor was washed, they all had to be folded and put out of the way.

So Emerson assigned a cleaning person to take care of the MH. The second individual to hold this position, Ted Williams, an English artist living in Boston and Cape Cod, soon joined the MH and became for several years an invaluable member. It was also necessary during the week to take down all the religious objects to be stored in a locked closet at the back of the auditorium, and then on Friday nights and Sunday mornings to put them back up. Ralph Edlund, (8) whose skill with tools did so much to make the MH function smoothly, built a cart with wheels to make this laborious task easier.(9)

The basic features of the Meeting House experiment were already well in place and functioning when I became a plain and ordinary member of the family. I soon understood, however, Ken's attraction to the small and loyal group who supported his creative efforts through financial thick and thin, through his ability to be insensitive and careless of human feelings,(10) and through the lack of any real support from the larger religious liberal community for their pilot program. First, they shared—each in his and her own way—the philosophical approach he articulated in address after address, in publication after publication and second, they saw the value in his ideas about music, art, and symbolism for liberal religion. Some from the very start of the MH, others more gradually through the learning process of listening to his words and ideas from week to week. Quite simply, sitting in his congregation on a regular basis, I found Ken to be the most stimulating, thoughtful, and instructive religious teacher and leader that I have had the privilege of encountering. This statement is not to ignore the many talented men and women in our liberal ministry. It is offered only as an example of why those who committed themselves to the Meeting House did so.

When Ken accepted the ministry of the Unitarian Society of Ridgewood in 1964, he did not abandon the Meeting House. For three years he came up on Thursday night, many times by bus, arriving in Boston about 5 A.M., held a service on Friday night, then took the bus back to Ridgewood and his service there on Sunday. It could not have been easy for him or his family. Typical of Ken, however, he thought of the Friday service as an experiment that might be useful to other congregations. Did we really need to gather only on Sundays? In many ways, what he tried the Roman Catholic churches have also tried—more successfully—with services on Saturday afternoon and night as well as on Sunday. Perhaps some of our UU churches, which have two services on Sunday morning, might look into Ken's experiment. The last full year of his MH connection he gave up the Friday experiment, however, and came up one Sunday a month to lead the service.

When Ken accepted me as his co-minister (at first the title was associate minister) it did not mean that he believed I was his equal in ability—although he never in any way suggested that I was not. Our relationship during the three years we worked together was warm and cooperative.(11) Unfortunately, as with others of the Meeting House family, when the connection was officially broken after 1968, the tie of friendship was not sustained.

My appointment came about because I was there, already a Meeting House member, without a job, and with a wife willing to live with two children in three rooms in a busy and noisy building on almost nothing. As for me, well, as Senator Lloyd Bentsen said to Vice President Dan Quayle, I can say: "I knew Ken Patton, and Alan, you're no Ken Patton." Nobody really was. That was the central reason why the Meeting House, despite good efforts and intentions, did not survive, once Ken had fully transferred his activity to Ridgewood.(12)

Fortunately, the newsletters put out by the Meeting House for the period 1965 through 1968 are preserved in the library of the Harvard Divinity School.(13) An examination of them gives a sense of the way the congregation attempted to carry on after Ken started to shift the main focus of his ministry to Ridgewood. In some ways, that carrying on was like playing on the Boston Red Sox baseball team after its owner sold off Babe Ruth to the New York Yankees in 1919. But the committed core group did make a valiant effort. Indeed, five years after Ken had cut his MH ties in 1968, Roland Hueston Jr. presented a motion to the board of trustees listing 20 items that needed their attention. The preface to his motion went: "I move that at the earliest possible date the church auditorium be restored to a condition for services for the celebration of life, the furthering of universal religion, and recognition of the religious, artistic and philosophic contributions of cultures of the world, past and present, such a setting being better for *any* type of meeting than the present disordered mess."(14)

It is obvious that Ken made his break at Boston with a great deal of reluctance. He spoke often about maintaining his relationship with the Meeting House and that it was a "continuity" which he prized. There is no indication that he had sought a change of venue; indeed, the Ridgewood opportunity just appeared out of nowhere, much as had his Boston call. Clearly the retiring minister at Ridgewood, Homer Sheffer, admired Ken, and felt that only Patton or Steve Fritchman could take his place at Ridgewood.

Fritchman, when queried, responded that he was too old to take on a new ministry; Ken, when asked, said he was interested. Obviously Ridgewood had many advantages for Ken. It was a strong humanist society and its retiring minister was as fiercely honest and independent, as was Patton. Further, in good ways and perhaps not-so-good ways, their personalities were similar. Finally, Ridgewood had a much larger congregation than Charles Street and, as a result, a more stable budget. If Boston had been the pilot experiment, Ridgewood would be the experiment.

So representatives came from Ridgewood to Boston to interview him and he went to Ridgewood to preach and meet the congregation. In April he was called, his services to begin as of July 1, 1964. In Doris B. Armstrong's admirable 1997 history of the Ridgewood Society, there is no reference to his continuing on at the Meeting House. Yet he did: for three years leading Friday evening services, and then for one year preaching in Boston the first Sunday of the month. In actual fact, his Boston ministry did not end in June 1964 but in June 1968.(15)

So what happened during those last four years at the Meeting House? Well, Ken did one of the things he did best: gave addresses that taught and expanded the mind of those listening and later of those who were to read his words. Without any question we in Boston were getting the same words as those in Ridgewood. No problem there. Here, gathered from the *Meeting House Messenger*, are some of them:

- "Small Majesties"—Every day we are surrounded by a thousand small majesties. If we notice them and fully appreciate them, our lives can never be mean or commonplace.

- "Do-It-Yourself Religion"—The liberal, if he is to fully exercise his religious freedom, must create his own religion, fashioned to the truth as he knows it, and to his own moral values.

- "To Define Equality"—Equality, as a principle of democracy and of humane life, is not an obvious principle. In what ways are people equal? What constitutes equal treatment of people, as different as we are from one another?"

- "The Impermissible"—Certain attitudes and acts become impermissible as civilization develops. The impermissible in the view of society are called crimes. Others become impermissible to the personal conscience.

- "A Bill of Rights for Children"—Children are the only group in our society not protected by civil rights. They are owned by their parents and are coerced and deprived of their freedoms.

Those were the subjects discussed on Friday nights; on Sunday mornings the visiting speakers, none of whom received even a token honorarium, included these individuals, with topics:

- "Miss America, *Playboy,* and the Berkeley Riots"—Dr. Dorothy Spoerl, editor, Department of Adult Programs, UUA.
- "Human Rights, Patients, and the Doctor"—Dr. Samuel Bachrach, director of the Arthritis Clinic, Memorial Hospital, Worcester, Massachusetts.
- "Dance and Other Activities"—Ann Tolbert, performed by the Dance Circle of the Boston Company and Toby Armour.
- "Religious Implications of the Mississippi Freedom Movement"—Rev. Donald A. Thompson, Minister for Social Responsibility, Benevolent Fraternity of Unitarian Churches.
- "Humanistic Religious Awareness"—Dr. Abraham H. Maslow, Professor of Psychology, Brandeis University.

Meanwhile, the MH continued to run and support many of its regular programs, such as the family dinner on the first Sunday of the month (with its amazing charge of adults $1.00, children 50 cents), Sunday programs for children, and the weekly work nights, now held on Thursday. This latter change meant that core members had to spend Thursday night, Friday night, and a good part of Sunday at the MH. As most also worked for a living, you can see what their devotion to the ideals of the MH meant to them. A lot was asked of them, and they gave a lot.

During these years, however, when Ken was only part-time at the MH, more than just keeping going was attempted. Besides loaning our exhibits to other churches, selling Meeting House Press books, and adding a few new art objects to the collection—an example was a black stone Celtic cross from Ireland, with primitive figure carvings and designs—new programs were dreamed up and tried. Some came from Ken, and some others had his blessing. But I fear not all of them did, and it was often difficult for him to practice his own teaching: "The lib‑eral, if he is to fully exercise his religious freedom, must create his own religion." To which might be added the single phrase: "and his own reli‑gious programs."

Patton continued to use the MH as a "laboratory" for further exper‑imental trials. One of these he described in the newsletter: "During the last few months, we have developed what we think is a successful 'ritual.' This involves the lighting of the atom and the lamp, with a musical back‑ground, and a reading related to the theme of the service. This sets the 'cosmic dimension' of the service." Ken also worked hard promoting the Institute of Creative Arts. He saw the Meeting House as its center in New England, Ridgewood as its center for the Middle Atlantic area, and hoped that other centers would soon develop throughout the country.

Patton's assessment of the MH to the UUA during the this period was this: "The society, as now constituted, stands as curator, custodian, and developer of the past projects, the symbol collection, the art collec‑tion, the library, the record library, the open hymnal, etc. As long as the Meeting House survives, its past activities will thus survive and develop." Later in this report he stated that the MH was "still the most varied and effective laboratory we have, in its field of specialization. It has a small, but committed membership. In its arrangement with Emerson College, it seems to have devised a means of keeping up repairs on the building and meeting utility and other expenses."(16)

In one of the most significant ventures of this period the Meeting House provided space in its building for the American Museum of Negro History. The location grew out of conversations with the co-ministers, the MH Board of Trustees, and Sue Bailey Thurman (Mrs. Howard Thurman), the driving forcing behind establishing the museum. At first there was concern among some members about the religious education program of the MH, since the children's room was to become the first home of the new museum, but this was resolved peaceably. To represent the MH family, I was elected to the new museum's board of directors and had the privilege to move its official formation. J. Marcus Mitchell was its first coordinator of exhibitions, and Dr. Nathan Huggins was its first president. "For the past two years," Dr. Huggins wrote on November 7, 1967, "the American Museum of Negro History has presented programs and exhibits at 70 Charles Street in Boston, where we have our headquarters. Our programs have included lectures on art, history, and literature. Last April we presented Langston Hughes in what sadly proved to be his last public appearance before his death. Since June, the Museum has had an exhibit of historical documents, first editions, and art which has been acclaimed to be the most significant presentation on Negro art and life in Boston's history. So far we have conceived of ourselves as creating a living museum illuminating the African seed in Boston's development, providing, thus, a richer and truer historical sense for all Bostonians, white and black."(17)

Even without Ken's direction (and sometimes without his approval), the MH family continued its tradition of sponsoring art programs and shows. For several years the MH ran the Charles Street Meeting House Bi-Annual Open Air Art Festival for Boston's Young Artists. A booklet was put out for the event, which described in some detail the Meeting House's mission as a setting "for a religion for one world, with displays of religious art and symbols of many cultures, ancient and modern."

These shows attracted many people and at one the judges included Clifford Ackley from the Museum of Fine Arts, Jan Cox, painter, scenic designer, and teacher; and Caron Le Brun, art critic for the *Herald Traveler*. One of the moving forces in these exhibits was the Meeting House's own artist, Ted Williams. Ted created many posters and announcements for the festivals and shows such as an exhibit drawn from our own collection of drawings and prints of Blake, Chagall, Daumier, and Goya, and Chinese drawings. Under the direction of Diane Pesso, a Children's Dance Company was initiated.

As well as these activities, under the management of Lee Eiseman and his crew, movies were shown Friday and Saturday evenings. These proved very popular with the young people living in the area and also caught the attention of the firemen stationed next to the MH. As a result there were several visits from the city inspectors to make sure that the building met all current public regulations, so there were even more tasks for the work night crew to attend. Lee Eiseman found an older gentleman who had played the piano in a local Boston motion picture house during the silent era. At his insistence we tried some silent films. These pre-talkies drew extralarge crowds, so at one Easter, Lee ran the uncut version of Cecil B. DeMille's *The King of Kings*. It was long, ever so long, and even presenting the final reel at double its normal running time, the organ motor was not shut off until 3 AM. Jean Seaburg knew this because in our apartment, our bed was against the wall on the other side of which was the organ motor.

For two years we opened the Meeting House on the evening before Christmas, always a special time on Beacon Hill. Several members of the MH family came early and put up the art centers in the sanctuary and Marie Lyons brought in several pine trees, which we placed before the front entrance to give the old Meeting House a festive feeling. Tours were given to those who stepped in, attracted by the pines and lighted windows. And wonderful Charlotte Edlund had prepared punch and a spread for them.

The Meeting House during these years did not stop its activities in the area of social justice. Beside the earlier mentioned relationship with the American Museum of Negro History, the MH called a press conference for the Boston media where its resident minister and Khoren Arisian, the leader of the Boston Ethical Society, spoke in favor of the work of Bill Baird, who had just been arrested at Boston University by officers from the state's vice squad for passing out birth control devices to students and for supporting a woman's right to have an abortion. The MH also opened its pulpit that Sunday morning to Mr. Baird.

So, during the years when Ken shared his ministry at Ridgewood with Boston, no one can justly say that the MH family did not try to carry on in a viable way and manner the concepts embedded in a religion for one world. Yes, in the end we failed, but we did try. We added about 40 new members, the membership growing from 108 in 1964 to 140 in 1968. (18) For a while we even had a student and his wife, Ira and Mary Nell Benoy, from Crane Theological School join our staff as Crane Associates to support the cause. Nevertheless, the average attendance at religious services was thirty-six and for the Church School ten.

Furthermore, there was always the problems of no budget, an inadequate and costly building to run, no endowment, and too few members sharing the workload. And in my case, a minister whose best talents were in other directions, so he was unable to provide the dynamic ideas and thrust that had sustained the loyalty of the basic Meeting House family during the Patton years. In 1968 I thought it was probably time for a change of leadership, so I left the MH, and, as it turned out, Ken also did so that summer.

The Meeting House, then, was to follow another pathway until its remaining members, no longer able to afford operating and maintaining the old building, left it in 1979 to carry on their activities elsewhere. Eventually that group just faded away. The UUA, which owned the building and had spent a lot of money on its upkeep over the years, put it on the market and sold it. (19) The amazing fact here, however, is that the Meeting House lasted as long as it did and that it accomplished so much during its lifetime, and not that it did not survive—as ministers like to say—for ever and ever.

But what a family was that Meeting House crowd! Let me give you an introduction to just one member, Anne Stedman. Here she is, in the words of the Rev. Richard Kellaway: "Our first meeting was at the Charles Street Meeting House in Boston in the 1950's. She was a member of this new, radical and innovative humanist Universalist congregation. Hardly typical for a lady of proper Boston background. Aunt Anne was always eager to explore new ideas and alternative pathways. She listened closely, encouraged creative interchange, acted independently. Three words express my experience of her—kindness, character, integrity."

Well, the whole darn Meeting House family was exactly like Anne Stedman. Don't let anyone ever claim that Ken Patton created the Meeting House. He did not. Indeed, he would not have lasted as long as he did in Boston, nor the Meeting House accomplish what it did, without Charlotte I. Edlund, Joseph K. Fish, Viola D. Pease, Roland A. Hueston Jr., Ralph Edlund and his family, Ruth H. Vickery, Virginia and Charles McCormick, Walter McDougall, Susan Bose, Ted Williams, Mary Lillie, Charlotte Fish, Charlotte Smith, and Marie and Wilson Lyons. (20) I have limited this list to those outside the profession of ministry, but there were special supporters in those ranks too. It was a team effort, in the best sense of that maligned term, and the Meeting House family was indeed a special family. Cheers, and a well-done, to every one of them!

Postscript

To try and see Kenneth Patton as a Universalist, and working in that thin and narrow confine, as some have done, is to evaluate his pilot experiment and effort within the field of religion, wrongly. Even if the term Unitarian is prefixed to that word Universalist, the essential Patton is missed, for he never intended that his version of a religion for one world be Unitarian Universalism expanded to absorb and include all other traditions under its banner.

The Unitarian Universalist Association then, used as a symbol of the eclectic tradition now called Unitarian Universalism, was never for Patton the birthing center from which the future shape of the religious impulse was to change and evolve further. At its best, it was a womb, a convenient one, but certainly not the only one available. Unfortunately, Unitarian Universalism in this matter never got beyond some false labor pains. There is no doubt that it failed Kenneth Patton's expectations and, just as clearly, there is no question but that it was not ready for the opportunity and the possibilities embedded and developed at the Charles Street Meeting House.

Another reason that this particular Meeting House experiment failed, in addition to the lack of response of Unitarian Universalism, was that it offered but one model for a world religion, and that model was contained and confined largely within the practice and thought of Protestant Christianity. One need look no further than the elements represented in its services and seasonal festivals. That liturgy, while it promoted the use of contemporary readings, music, and art, as well as those of past generations, hung from a worship structure identified most closely with just one pattern of worshipping,(20) and that one has lost its value for most current *Homo sapiens.*

A question that those at the Meeting House never thought very deeply about is this: will a religion, understanding as we do the make up of the mind of *Homo sapiens*, it is more useful to say, will the religions of the future, be described by concepts such as church, synagogue, temple? Furthermore, will people even desire such institutions to be connected to their thinking, pondering, and deciding about how they conduct their living? Indeed, will they care, outside of academic conversation and museum visiting, about incorporating into their personal religions the arts and rituals of other religious attempts? Finally, when people understand the philosophical implications contained in the concept of evolution aright, will their responses and solutions, no matter how temporary, reflect in any real degree those familiar to older world cultures?

Take, as but one example, marriage, where even people who live outside the current religious communities turn to either religious or state officials, to become legally a committed couple. Will this continue as the norm? Does the state or religion have any real say here? The answer will soon be: No. If swans that usually make lifelong pair bonds do not need any celebratory service, any legal document to mate and raise their offspring, why then, outside of historical precedent and traditions, are *Homo sapiens* any different? In the end, the decision to live with another or not to continue to live with another is as personal and private as the decision to have or not have a child. It exists outside the validity of both government and of any formalized religious communities.

At all three of his UU parishes, Patton operated within the philosophy of religious humanism. It was in that garden that he grew his different flowers and vegetables, or "pilot experiments." He realized that they were "pilot" seeds but probably did not completely envision that many would soon be outdated baggage, would soon—perhaps—be replaced by even more beautiful and fragrant varieties. For *Homo sapiens* in the last century, called the twentieth, took—in the image of the first walkers on the moon—a giant step. In this instance as with those steps on the moon— forward and not backwards—although both directions are, at any given historical period, possible. Our understanding of the way things are, the way they really work, will never be content to return to the first myths and fables, and the want-to-be, of all previous generations of the species. One of the accomplishments of the Meeting House, at least within the tradition of a more liberal religious understanding of facts, is that it proudly proclaimed—and meant—our universal condition as one species on one planet.

A nagging matter that remains when considering Patton's contributions is this: did he really believe that the physical setup of the worship space of the Meeting House, and its adornment with the older religious symbols and art, would be adopted generally by his chosen association of churches and fellowships? A careful examination of the book *A Religion for One World*, which was his most important discussion of the concept, indicates that he did.(22) Although there were some churches and ministers who, to some degree, picked up on his ideas, most did not, and probably never will. What he thought about this, during his last years at Ridgewood, would be interesting to know.(23)

Another nagging question is this: if Patton had not left Madison for Boston, would his ministry—and for him that was the construct of the pilot experiment at the Meeting House—have been any different? I do not believe so. What he attempted in Boston could just as well have been attempted at Madison, as it was, to a lesser degree, in Ridgewood. That he left Boston for the economic stability of the Unitarian Society in Ridgewood, as well as its strong humanist tradition, is most understandable. But why he left his apparently flourishing ministry at the Madison Meeting House just as it was in the midst of planning its Frank Lloyd Wright building which was based on ideas Patton believed in is hard to fathom. Certainly a ministry there would have been as exciting and challenging as one in Boston. Further, it does not seem reasonable to conclude that the experiments undertaken here could not have been made in Madison.

What, then, was Patton's major contribution to the future development of the concepts we label as religion? Obviously it is what he wrote—be it his philosophical addresses and books or his worship materials: hymns, readings, poetry. Indeed, during his twenty-two-year ministry at Ridgewood, the major emphasis of his work became writing, and more writing, which supports this conclusion. In his adopted Unitarian Universalist tradition, he stands with such past humanist thinkers as Curtis

Reese, John Dietrich, Charles Francis Potter, and A. Eustace Haydon. Outside of that tradition, he stands with such philosophers, but of course to a much lesser degree, as John Dewey, Bertrand Russell, and Alfred North Whitehead. As a producer of worship resources, he is one of many, both within Unitarian Universalist circles (for example, Hosea Ballou and Samuel Longfellow) and within the larger religious community.

Perhaps Ken Patton, without quite realizing that he was doing so, best evaluated his own accomplishments and ministry when he wrote: "We are a very young religion, without the rituals and traditions of most of the other religions of the world. We are still seeking our true voice and our rightful manner in celebration. This we cannot find without experiments in worship." He was one of those in the twentieth century trying to discover "our true voice and our rightful manner." There were others, and there will continue to be others. That's the way it is with *Homo sapiens!* I believe that Kenneth Patton and the people of the Charles Street Meeting House would find membership in this category an appropriate and honest historical judgment about their life efforts.

Notes

1. See the Charles Street Meeting House files at the UUA Archives, 25 Beacon Street, Boston., for Dana McLean Greeley to Kenneth L. Patton, Letter, June 22, 1964, and Kenneth L. Patton to Ray Hopkins, Letter, January 7, 1966.
2. This condemnation also censures my own lack of vision for as a young delegate, representing the First Universalist Church of Medford at the Massachusetts Universalist Convention meeting in Haverhill in 1951, I voted against funding the Meeting House.

    When thinking about MH funding, it is vital to remember that financial support for its activities often came from sources outside of the regular budget. For example, Corliss Lamont's helping to fund its press.

    The best account to date of the early struggles of the Meeting House to survive as an institution, but still just a sketchy one, is found in Charles A. Howe, "He Lives Tomorrow: Clinton Lee Scott, Revitalizer of Universalism," *Proceedings of the Unitarian Universalist Historical Society*, 21 (1989) 7-25. In addition, there is helpful material concerning the Meeting House in the archival files of the Massachusetts Universalist Convention (bMS 346) and of the Universalist Historical Society (bMS 202) at the Andover-Harvard Theological Library, Harvard Divinity School.

I should add one additional note: I was one of those who journeyed to the Meeting House on 6 February 1949 to see Ken installed. I was crowded in the back corner of the right balcony. Sad to admit, I do not recall a thought contained in his address. But I do remember that he did not wear a robe; it was the first time I had ever seen a minister at a service without one. I was also surprised that he gave the main address himself. (You can see how naive I was.) The strongest memory of that occasion, however, was that during his talk the top half of one of those old church windows was suddenly pulled down its track by gravity and hit bottom with a loud boom. It was, of course, chance, but how appropriate.

3.   These rooms for several reasons (chiefly financial) eventually became a "parsonage" for the MH. What is intriguing about this fact is that when Frank Lloyd Wright was designing the Meeting House he built for the Madison Unitarian Society, Ken as the minister insisted that the building include "a residence for the minister." Wright agreed, but when Ken "abruptly resigned his post to accept a new position in Boston" the next minister in Madison, Frederick L. Cairns, declared that he would never live in a church. His negative stance eventually eliminated the idea from the plan. So it was not until after he had been in Boston for several years that Patton came to live in a church. For Patton's ideas for what he called the "Church of Tomorrow" and for his role in the planning of Wright's second UU church see Mary Jane Hamilton, *The Meeting House: Heritage and Vision*, Madison, Wisconsin., Friends of the Meeting House, 1991.

4.   While I was chair of the board, the Pattons had Jean and me to supper one evening. It was a delightful repast and was followed by real conversation, for we discussed religion and unmet political needs. The apartment had but three rooms: two bedrooms and a combined general area with the kitchen in one corner. After the meal, the table had been cleared and the dirty dishes piled in the sink. As we talked, Ken kept glancing at those dishes and then at Mitzi. She ignored the matter. Finally, Ken began suggesting that she wash them. She still ignored the matter. At last he got up, still holding forth with his views on various topics, and did the dishes. I never saw Mitzi react to his deed, but years later I understood more, for when my brother spent a weekend with them at Ridgewood he noticed that Mitzi had an upstairs room that was called, to use Virginia Woolf's lovely phrase, a room of one's own.

5.   Some summers when the Seaburgs were in Vermont the flat was sublet. For example, Ernest and Beverly Cassara stayed there in 1967 while Beverly was studying at Boston University for her doctorate in education. This is but one example of how the MH had to constantly to find ways to raise additional money in order to plug its often-leaky budget.

6.   The two individuals, Al and Diane Pesso, who directed the college's dance program at this period were also members of the MH.

7.   Kitty, our rather large black-and-white cat, made himself a familiar figure to teachers and students, for it was his wont to stroll about these rows of chairs during lectures. Late in the afternoon, when there were no more classes, my daughters played

there. Ted Williams fondly remembers Ann bouncing a blue ball there. She was also happy to let her Slinky toy climb down the long curving front steps.

8. Ralph often worked with his sidekick at the MH, Walter McDougall, who lived in Lynn but was a regular at the Friday night work parties. One day a fire inspector visited the MH and told me that we had to fix the fire escape at the back of the building. I told Ralph about the matter. He looked at me, smiled, and with his eyes twinkling, said, "Don't worry about the fire department. The firm of Edlund and McDougall will take care of the problem." And they did!

9. This process worked without a hitch for several years. Then one Sunday Roland Hueston Jr., the long-time treasurer and librarian of the Meeting House, who had assumed the job of putting up the religious art for each service, discovered, to his horror, when he opened the closet one Sunday in the 1970s that it was bare. He reported this fact to the minister and the board; if any action was ever taken to recover the art is unknown. Hueston did write to Ken telling him about the missing art collection but never heard from him on the subject. It was at this point that Roland, one of the MH's most loyal supporters, sadly resigned his membership. (Source: Conversation with Roland Hueston Jr., Spring 2000.)

    Fortunately, some years earlier, after Ken had gone to Ridgewood, the Meeting House congregation, at an annual meeting, had voted to present him with some of the art held "in storage." A few of these pieces, along with the collection of sixty-five religious symbols that had adorned the auditorium (they had been made by Charlotte Edlund, her brother Ralph, and Ken), eventually found their way, most appropriately, to the Starr King School for the Ministry at Berkeley, California.

10. I am not sure that Ken ever realized how much pain some of his remarks caused members of the MH family. And, I must add, I never once heard him say that he was sorry for what he had said.

    While on this subject, let me note that many UUs have declared that one of the reasons for the failure of the Meeting House to survive as an institution was Ken's personality. Obviously, it created problems for the Society, but how much of a real role it played in the inability of the MH to realized the highly unrealistic hopes of its founders needs more solid documentation—if it exists—than has been offered so far.

11. "I would like to take this opportunity to personally welcome Alan Seaburg as Associate minister of the Meeting House. He and his family are occupying the apartment, and the Meeting House seems like a much warmer place with a family living in it again." Kenneth Patton, *Meeting House Messinger*, September 24, 1965. In addition, at my request, on several occasions he took the time to critique my essays and poetry. I found that his suggestions were always helpful.

12. One of the reasons, but obviously not the chief one, that Ken continued to come to Boston from New Jersey, was, as he explained it to me, his reluctance to burn all his bridges as he had done when he moved from Madison to Boston. Clearly, by 1968, he no longer needed his Boston "bridge." He felt, and rightly, that his role and

work at Ridgewood were secure.

13. See at Harvard Divinity School, Mflm Unit 55, *Meeting House Messenger*, 1965–1968. Unfortunately, earlier issues are yet to be located, as is also true for most of the official record books kept by the MH. The Divinity School does have, however, some further archival documents, many of them papers relating to Meeting House financial matters. See at its library bMS 399 and bMS 528. At Patton's death, several boxes of his own papers were donated to the library of the Meadville/Lombard Theological School in Chicago.

14. His motion, which was made November 12, 1973, can be found in its entirety at the Andover-Harvard Theological Library. See bMS 399.

15. See especially chapter 6, "Space for Universal Religion, 1964–1986," in Doris B. Armstrong, *Unitarians in Ridgewood: 100 Years of Freedom, Community, and Concern.* Ridgewood, NJ: The Unitarian Society, 1997. This excellent history delineates the Patton ministry openly and honestly. The interviews with the members of those years add depth and feeling to the historical account. Patton and the congregation are revealed as a collection of human beings capable of making mistakes and of reaching for glory.

16. See Kenneth L. Patton to Ray Hopkins, Letter, January 7, 1966, UUA Archives, Boston.

17. The museum is now known as the Museum of Afro American History. It is housed in the African Meeting House, just off Joy street, on Beacon Hill, which the museum purchased in 1972. See Robert C. Hayden, *The African Meeting House in Boston*, Boston: Museum of Afro American History, 1987.

18. Statistics are from the *UUA Directory, 1964–1969*. The budget also rose from 6,500 in 1964 to 11,750 in 1968.

19. The UUA had had good offers for the building as early as 1964 but it waited until the congregation vacated the premises before selling it. See Dana McLean Greeley to Kenneth L. Patton, June 22, 1964.

20. I am sorry for those who belong here who I have omitted. For this, I plead a "senior moment." To appreciate the personality of Marie Lyons and to learn why she became a Universalist in the first place, see *The Christian Leader*, 133 (1951) 152.

21. Indeed, for a while Patton even talked about developing a liberal religious mass.

22. See especially pp. 382–385.

23. It may have been bitter. When the MH congregation and its minister in 1973 considered selling the Kollwitz prints to meet expenses—and it did so in 1977 through a local art dealer—Ken wrote the then President of the UUA, Robert West, that "to have the art collection and the other facets of the projects destroyed in the death of the church, to pay the bills of a defunct organization, is most bitter for me, and I should think for the movement, which subsidized the Meeting House and its projects. The loss will be yours as well as mine." Kenneth L. Patton to Robert West, Letter, April 30, 1973, UUA Archives, Boston.

More eloquently he wrote a letter to Roland Hueston Jr. to be read to the congregation considering the sale: "Kollwitz was one of our own. Her father and grandfather were liberal ministers. She was an artistic prophet of liberal religion, of humanity, freedom, motherhood, the advancement of the working class, the end of peasantry, the condemnation of war, compassion for death. The collection is a great and powerful preachment of our essential message and concerns. If we have any essential religious art, this is it. It should be a permanent art treasure of our movement and so it was intended . . . to take them from liberal religion, which is already so naked of art and symbol would be a desecration." Kenneth L. Patton to Roland Hueston, Jr., Letter, undated, UUA Archives, Boston.

Section III

Philosophy and Critique

Chapter 10

Art and Symbols for a Universal Religion

Kenneth L. Patton

Eight years ago the Universalists in Massachusetts were faced with the paradoxical situation of having no Universalist church in the city of Boston, which is the home of the state and national headquarters. Due to shifts in population and other pressures, twenty-two Universalist churches had perished. A widening ring of suburbs around the city was also being stripped.

The Massachusetts Universalist Convention, under the leadership of its Superintendent, Dr. Clinton Lee Scott, decided to establish a new Universalist church in Boston as an extension project. The historic Charles Street Meeting House was secured as its home, and extensive repairs and redecoration were done.

Since traditional Universalism had fared poorly in Boston, it was the decision that the new church should be set up as a "pilot project" where experiments in church organization and services might serve to attract the liberal and pioneering people of the Greater Boston area. What has come to be known as "The Meeting House Project" is now almost eight years old. It has been truly experimental, in that only a general idea of direction and content existed in the beginning.

Religion has been concerned mainly with treasuring the past. It is mostly authoritarian and traditional, locating its authority in divine revelation, great teachers, a Golden Age, holy books, and its priests have been the custodians and conservators of the traditional rites and laws. For this and other reasons, experimentation, pioneering and invention fare poorly in religious institutions, whereas they have become accepted practice in other fields. John Dewey has pointed out that the great invention was "the invention of invention." The Meeting House has attempted to apply this approach to religion, setting up an experimental laboratory in religious arts, symbols, organization, services and program.

The basic innovation has been in the nature of the religious community itself. The Meeting House has become a continuous family work project. But the work is not primarily money-raising activities, such as church dinners, fairs, and bake sales, and the program is not primarily social, such as teas, card parties, treasure-hunts, "programs." Each Friday evening there is a "work night." The Meeting House is a workshop. Those members who really enter into the Meeting House spirit, and not all do, of course, find an area of creative labor and self-expression. Only when we cannot design and build the things ourselves do we buy ready-made and hire outside help. Since many of the things we are after have never been made before, they could not be purchased ready-made in any case. Since to have them custom-made would be very expensive, and we do not have the money, we either have to make them ourselves or do without. Even if we could hire them done, I do not believe we would. We have discovered that the best part of a religious fellowship is doing things ourselves and doing them together.

The people at the Meeting House come from all manner of background, occupation, and social class. They hold one thing in common: a sense of eagerness to try out new ideas. There is a great potential of zest for experimentation and pioneering in most people that the churches have been missing, simply because they have not cultivated it. Churches have sold the people short on the prophetic and experimental side of religion. Most ministers and church leaders are afraid to try anything "different" or "radical." But religion does not have to be timid and conventional; we make ourselves after the image and the role we have chosen for ourselves. Most people will work and sacrifice far beyond ordinary expectations if they can find a dream large enough to capture them.

The Meeting House has one basic and simple idea: to find a religious setting for a religion of one humanity and one world. It is the United Nations idea, especially as it is embodied in UNESCO, applied to religion. Our unofficial motto comes from Torrence: "I am a man, and nothing that is human can be alien to me." We are a completely free-mind fellowship, with no creed or confession of faith. We look for insight and wisdom to all of humanity, for truth and goodness have never been the monopoly of any one people or religion. For this reason we do not call ourselves Christian or Jewish or Buddhist, although these traditions are greatly cherished along with the others.

We include all and exclude none, for only thus can we be positive and nonexclusive in our approach.

This, however, does not mean that we are uncritical: quite the opposite. The criteria of evidence reasonableness and consistency are applied to all. The scientific method and attitude, along with the findings of the various branches of science, are allied to the arts, to philosophy and to "naturalistic mysticism," to give us a religious approach that is at once hard-headed and tough-minded, and appreciative and warm-hearted. Belief is allied with doubt, affirmation with criticism. We reject all creeds and dogmas on principle, for only when the open mind is free to probe and discover can it accept the other person's faith as part of the human scene, and appreciate it without accepting it as adequate for our own use. To criticize is not to reject. This point must be emphasized, for it is the dividing line between the free mind and fanaticism. It is the doorway to a universal religion that rigorously seeks the truth, and yet is also inclusive and welcoming to all.

What are the fundamental symbols for such a universal religion? The United Nations found its symbol in the world encircled with the olive wreath of peace. The symbols which we have chosen and created are of several kinds. What are the core realities of the human situation? How can they be symbolized?

First is the universe itself, from which our name "universal" is taken. The universe is symbolized in two ways: in a "stellar globe" which gives the constellations of both the northern and southern hemispheres, and makes an attractive luminous sphere when lighted at night. At the front of the auditorium in an arch which is fifteen feet wide and twenty-five high, we have reproduced the Great Nebula in Andromeda from astronomical photographs. This nebula is our next-door neighbor in space, practically a twin of the Milky Way Nebula of which our solar system is a part. It gives us a "window into the universe," and provides us with the key for our cosmic orientation since this nebula is seen through a screen of stars in our own galaxy. We call it a "symbol of the fact." It is a photographic reproduction. Each person is left make his own interpretation of this reality. He can say: "The heavens declare the glory of God," or "The heavens declare the glory," or he can just say, "My heavens!" Another astronomic scene, the Horse's Head Nebula in the constellation of Orion, a portion of our own galaxy, is painted on one of the walls downstairs.

The earth is symbolized by a large polar-projection map of the earth inlaid in linoleum in the very center of the auditorium. All national boundaries are eliminated, giving the one land mass, the one earth. Around this is a golden circle, which we have chosen as the master-symbolism of Universalism. The circle is found in all cultures, and has variously symbolized the universe, the sun, the moon, the earth, unity, perfection, holiness, peace. The earth within the circle is repeated downstairs, with the symbols of the world religions inscribed upon it at the point of their origin.

The pews have been rearranged to face in four banks toward the center, coming in from the four corners of the room. Thus the people, being seated in a circle, symbolize unity and one world in their very arrangement. "Religion in the round" is also a symbol of democracy, since the people face one another, and not the altar. The minister and the choir sit in the pews with the congregation, and the preaching is done from the edge of the map in the inner circle.

Hanging from the ceiling opposite the mural is a "construction" which is an allegorical symbol of the microcosm, the atom, the cell, the seed. This is the work of Jack Burnham, a young Boston artist, who designed and executed it and gave it to the Meeting House as his contribution to the project. The center of it is lighted, and the mural of the nebula is painted in "black light," and gives a very close representation of the night sky. When the construction and the mural, microcosm and macrocosm, are lighted in an otherwise darkened room, the position of man, who in size and complexity is about halfway between the two, is effectively symbolized.

In time we plan to have a large bas-relief sculpture in the arch opposite the mural of the nebula, symbolizing humanity. This might be a single figure, or a family scene. Man is otherwise symbolized in art, in photographs, paintings, sculpture and etchings. But the large symbol of man is still for the future.

On the platform at the front is a large bookcase which houses the major writings of all the world cultures and religions. Whereas dogmatic religions sometimes put "the one book" front center, we put the many great books of mankind together as a symbol of our acceptance of all human wisdom and poetry and literature as ours. A smaller bookcase beside it houses the Torah, the Megillah, and Buddhist texts inscribed on leaves made from palm. We will add an original Koran and other books in their native languages and styles of publication.

On the bookcase is a lamp made from Greek and Roman design, which is a symbol of light, life, wisdom, the hearth, the home, and aspiration. The lamp is lighted at the beginning of the service and snuffed at the close.

The use of the high-fidelity sound system is another symbol, for we have a collection of the music of the world cultures, which is used as a background for readings from the various cultures.

Alongside these core symbols is the symbol project itself. As a whole, it too is a core symbol, since it is made up of some sixty-five symbols taken from the world religions, ancient and modern, and symbols of the "universals," of the common ideals, goals, and occupations of humanity. These symbols adorn the panels on the facing of the balconies, and two panels to either side of the mural of Andromeda. The designing, research, and execution of these symbols took five years. They are made of brass, copper, and silver, and the metalwork was done by a brother and sister, Charlotte and Ralph Edlund.

The whole of the auditorium of the Meeting House has been made into one integrated symbol. The map of the earth in the center is the key.

If you draw a line from the North Pole at the center outwards, it will lead you, say, across Japan, then to the symbols of Japan on the balcony, and behind them to a space between the windows on the outer wall where the art of Japan is located. Thus "centers" of the art of the world religions form the outer ring, within which the people meet. Beginning at the front to the right, the "centers" in order are Oceania, Japan, China, Tibet, India, Buddhism, Oriental Universalism, Egypt, Africa, Islam, Judaism, Christianity, Aztec, American Indian cultures. There will be another ring of centers in the balcony for some of the auxiliary cultures, such as Greece, Rome, Babylonia, Parsees, Stone Age, Confucianism, Taoism. Large wall hangings are planned for the four corners. Already we have a large Tree of Life Persian rug, on loan from the Universalist Church of America, and in time hangings from India, China, and Mexico will be added.

The collection of the art of the world religions has been our major occupation for the last year and a half, and has progressed far beyond our expectations. Some major gifts have been received, and great personal sacrifice on the part of various members of the Meeting House has made other purchases possible. Excellent cooperation has been forthcoming from art dealers and collectors, and we have only begun to explore the possibilities.

The arts are the voices of humanity. Through sculpture, painting, music, literature, the dance, drama, and architecture, men communicate their most profound thoughts and emotions to one another. The arts always have been, and always will be, peculiarly the language of religion. Through the use of these communications from the many branches of humanity, past and present, we hope to assemble a truly universal setting or "frame of reverence" for our universalist celebrations. It is our hope that the composers, painters, sculptors, dancers, dramatists, and musicians of Boston will join us to find, through the expressions of the arts, a religious voice for our age.

As for music, the century-old organ is used primarily to accompany the congregational singing. Mrs. Harned Cushing has generously contributed her services for many years. The grand piano is used to accompany the choir on occasion, but the choir usually sings *a cappella*. Dr. Paul Giuliana contributes his services to rehearse the choir, and the singers are all unpaid volunteers. The high-fidelity sound system permits us to use the classical music of the West and the recorded music of all the cultures. A service is often built around a symphony, a chamber music work, or a great choral work. The first movement is used for a prelude, sometimes the andante section is played beneath the meditation, and the closing movements become the postlude. Music from China will be played as background to readings from China. This "unlocks" music for us, giving us limitless musical resources.

Much work has been done in collecting and creating anthems and hymns for a universal religion. The "open hymnal" is a spring-back folder in which a new hymnal is assembled each Sunday, with just the materials for that service arranged in order. Dr. Giuliana has done some original composition, but a great deal more is needed. A hymnal and an anthem series will be published by Meeting House Press in time; in the meantime this material is mimeographed.

Opening Services, Responsive Readings, Closing Sentences, Meditations, and other "worship materials" have been written and compiled from the literature of the world religions. Most of this is available in the two books just published that will be described below.

Experimental types and orders of service are the order, rather than the exception. We still do not believe that we have found the native atmosphere and approach to the "celebration of life." A series of celebrations is developing as experiments to this end. "Mid-Winter Festival," the first of the "Meeting House Services," will be published this winter.

In order to expedite our activities in this area, the Meeting House Press was established as the publishing agency of the Meeting House. Its first venture was a series of pamphlets with mimeographed text and printed covers. These were followed by a list of printed leaflets, *Universalist Definitions*, a magazine, *The Edge*, which in the future will become a printed pamphlet series. This change does not alter the purpose of *The Edge*, but does remove the pressure of regular issues. Four books have been published: *Worship and a Well Ordered Life*, by Clarence R. Skinner, and *Man Is the Meaning*, by Kenneth L. Patton. These books were published in collaboration with the Universalist Historical Society. Also by Mr. Patton are *Man's Hidden Search, an Inquiry into Naturalistic Mysticism*, and *Readings for the*

Celebration of Life. The latter contains the various readings created and compiled for use in the services, and is designed for use by other congregations. It is also available in loose-leaf form for those who wish to try the "open hymnal" approach. *Man Is the Meaning* is a manual for the use of worship leaders.

After each service there is a coffee hour and discussion period lasting for an hour, in which the issues of the address are freely argued. Regular adult study groups meet every Wednesday evening, studying such things as anthropology, psychology, comparative religion, and world politics. The Charles Street Forum brings in outside speakers on all kinds of social, political, theological, and other issues. Programs of social and legislative action are embarked upon through the Social Action Committee. At the monthly social evenings, there are dinners with the menus chosen from various lands, with speakers and films relating to the different cultures. Groups are made up to attend the theatre, forums, and gallery talks. We plan a continuous and varied program of adult education and action.

We have only a few children because of our downtown location, but an active program in nursery, kindergarten and some older groups is carried on, as numbers permit. The approach is a progressive, project method, with one of the most interesting projects conducted by Dr. Clyde Kluckhohn of Harvard University, in adapting the study of anthropology for ten to twelve-year-olds.

The next publication of Meeting House Press will be *Art and Symbols for a Universal Religion*, which will give a complete and illustrated summary of the Meeting House Project. This should be published next spring. The photography for the book and this article has been done by Charles McCormick and Peter Rossiter as their contribution to our work projects. Three sets of color transparency slides with legends are available from the Visual Education Department of the Council of Liberal Churches on the symbol project, the religious art of the West, and the religious art of the East.

Of course we take for granted being a non-segregated church on racial and cultural lines. Our members come from many racial and national and religious backgrounds. But we also try to be nonsegregated on sex and age levels. We have no men's and women's groups, nor youth and young adult divisions. Our meetings, education program, social affairs are for *everyone*, regardless of age or sex. This we believe is democracy in action. Our only exception is in the need for special educational programs for children.

I have not even begun to name the persons whose contributions in time, labor and money have made our project possible. They do janitorial and secretarial jobs, build furniture, wash and paint walls, teach, sing, compose, print, gather, staple and bind books and leaflets, sort type, cook—you name it. Because of all the work we do together, we have the feeling and fellowship of a family, and the coffee snack following the work night provides some of our best fellowship.

We try to be an experimental and creative free-mind community. We see the Universalist church as an attempt to establish an idealistic world community in miniature. We are not willing to wait a thousand years for universal religion and the brotherhood of man to come over all the earth. We do what we can, and attempt to bring it into reality in our small fellowship, hoping it will then have some small influence in bringing world brotherhood and the commonwealth of man into reality among all mankind and in every nation.

Chapter 11

The Charles Street Meeting House: The Setting for the Development of a Naturalistic Philosophy of Religion

Paul Sawyer

Fifty years ago, Kenneth Patton, an energetically brilliant, 38-year-old, tested minister was brought to Boston by the Universalist leadership. The Massachusetts Universalist Convention and the Universalist Church of America, led by Clinton and Mary Scott and Horton and Lynette Colbert, brought Patton there to initiate a ministry at newly created Charles Street Meeting House, housed in an historic church building purchased by the Massachusetts Convention. The purpose was to reestablish Universalism in Boston where its former churches had closed, and furthermore, to introduce a contemporary humanistic outlook and worship where none existed in the Boston area.

No one could have been more suited to this purpose than Kenneth Patton, a poet and intellectual with strong motivation. He had been minister at the First Unitarian Church of Madison, Wisconsin, where he had been instrumental in engaging Frank Lloyd Wright to design his first and only Unitarian Church. Coming out of a Disciples of Christ background, he had studied with liberal theologians such as Scribner Ames, Henry Nelson Weiman, and A. Eustace Haydon at the University of Chicago.

Then, after a ministry in the Disciples of Christ, he was called to the humanist congregation at Madison where his teacher Eustace Haydon had served before him.

Already Patton was a committed humanist in the tradition of the "Humanist Manifesto" of 1933 (signed by his mentor Eustace Haydon and the man who would bring him to Charles Street Universalist Meeting House, Clinton Lee Scott). As a younger man and poet, Patton already had shown an interest in the use of the arts for religious expression. In a sermon given at Madison entitled "The Myth of Love," he developed a bold concept which contributed an emotional depth to the then-current humanism. He started with the myth of Plato from *The Symposium*, where man and woman were originally one being and then divided. From that time they were attracted to one another and had the urge to come together again. Patton extrapolates from this love connection between human beings to the energy of mutual attraction that operates throughout the universe, from solar and galactic gravitation to the attraction between electrons and protons within the atom. The whole energy of existence, what brings it into being and keeps it in the living process, is love, he asserts. This is a far-reaching concept, akin to ideas in the *Kabbalah* and to those of the writer of John's letters in the New Testament. It is most appropriate for a poet. Interestingly enough, it is also akin to the traditional emphasis of American Universalism, which stressed the centrality of God's love and the fundamental prerequisite of love in human relations (Hosea Ballou and the Pauline emphasis among Universalists such as De Benneville). This emphasis upon love and emotional expression in poetry and the arts was to evolve further at the Charles Street Meeting House after Patton arrived there in 1949. He announced in his first publication of many to come: "A New Bottle, Worship and Symbolism for Universal Religion":

> The Charles Street Universalist Meeting House has been designated a "pilot project church" by the Massachusetts Universalist Convention and the Department of Education of the Universalist Church of America. This means that it has the function of setting up experiments in various fields . . . .

> After a year and a half of study, planning and con-
> struction, the pilot project on worship and symbolism is
> reaching maturity. . .
>
> Is it possible to create a form of worship so wide in
> its humanity, so inclusive in its symbolism, its resources in
> art, literature, and music that it can encompass the whole
> drama of mankind's religious quest? This we have set as
> our goal as a "universalist" church.

Patton and his working group of cutting-edge Universalists not only were interested in a new humanistic religious expression in words and concept. Equally important to them was to translate this perspective into ritual expression using contemporary universal worship forms. Given the conservative Christian nature of New England Unitarianism and Universalism at that time, the radical thrust of the Meeting House Project is easy to imagine.

Basic to Patton's artistic expression was one of the oldest and most universal means of religious knowing: what is referred to as "mystical experience." Patton quotes his own teacher, Eustace Haydon, who writes that the mystic experience is neutral in matters of belief, that folks bring out of these experiences what they bring to them. If they are theistic, they come out with a stronger sense of God's presence. If they are Buddhist, they experience nothingness and nirvana and letting go of desire, and so forth. For Kenneth Patton, the mystical experience is totally natural, the stuff of poetry and poetic awareness. Out of it comes a knowledge of the oneness of all existence, the interconnection of our bodies and the long body of the universe, the saga of the one human family and all cousin forms of life on this unique planet.

It is worth quoting Patton, for this emphasis upon natural mysticism is one of his contributions to contemporary religious humanism. It is often neglected by many so-called humanists, leaving their faith overly rational and emotionally thin. It allows critics of religious humanism, who do not know its full dimensions, to typify it as lacking spirit and depth.

> The same mysticism that [humanity] once used to escape
> the . . . flesh into a realm of pure spirituality . . . can now

(be) used to explore and occupy the magnificent realms of
the human spirit . . .

For [humankind] is also the mystical animal, the artis-
tic and poetic animal. [Humankind] is the religious animal.
(*Man's Hidden Search, an Inquiry into Naturalistic Mysticism*,
Boston, 1954, p. 109)

Here we have a melding of the ancient religious experience of
humans with our contemporary wonder and awe in the face of our
expanding knowledge of this one natural existence of which we are a
part. Patton takes the naturalistic breakthrough into the spirit of Unitarian
Universalist Transcendentalists such as Emerson, Thoreau, and Fuller and
translates it into down-to-earth everyday language.

There are moments when the sheerest and simplest sen-
sual experience wears a golden significance. Suddenly, as
the air is crystal clear after rain, objects take on a naked,
transparent meaning. We are probed and wounded by the
smooth, chill surface of glass, by a flashing sword of
color, by the explosive individuality of a bird or child. We
are stabbed by the is-ness and that-ness of things, and
there comes a fresh and splendid sense of existence. We
are shocked into self-awareness. . . . (*Ibid.*, p. 105)

Patton is writing this in 1954, before all the now-easily-available,
influential Eastern religious texts. Zen was an exotic, barely known religion. Thoreau was hardly read. Even poetry readings were unknown
outside of esoteric Manhattan occasions. All of these were influences
upon Kenneth who read (and wrote) voraciously and widely in all possible religious, poetic texts. He was an avatar of a developing universal
religious perspective that is now such a widespread cutting edge, that it
is taken for granted.

There can be no separation between natural and religious
mysticism. The experience of nature and human nature is

religious experience. . . .

In the mystical experience the whole person is gathered into an integration of intense awareness. All our senses are focused on the present scene. (*Ibid.*, p. 117)

Patton is clear that this kind of mystical experience—the source of our religious awareness—does not come from some other realm of the supernatural, nor does it transport us out of our bodies into a spiritual realm divorced from this everyday life.

In fact, he states that the spirit and imagination are part of this material nature, that the mind and soul are not separate from the body. Rather they are the "effervescence" of material nature.

> All is matter: neutrons, protons, atoms,
> > molecules, liquids, solids, dust, and flesh.
> Matter is no longer inane and gross;
> > it is everything . . .
> Spirit was a misnamed function of matter,
> > the mind, love, and life of the flesh.
> Matter is energy, light, heat, electricity,
> > electromagnetism, cosmic waves, and gravity.
> We can not escape the mantle of flesh into the spirit,
> > escape life and process into Nirvana,
> > > heaven and immortality.
> ("The Reality of Matter," *A Religion of Realities*, 1977,
> Meeting House Press, Ridgewood, New Jersey, p. 13.)

"Nature is everything that is," Patton writes—giving a name to the whole works of existence, which often in traditional Western religion has been named "GOD." Instead, Patton relegates the GOD word to the old-fashioned childhood use of that word as a personal God who speaks and acts and communicates in the world. Patton uses the word "Nature" to describe the whole business, revealing his kinship to Emerson who wrote his breakthrough transcendentalist religious work in 1836 with that title—although Emerson and Patton's own teacher, Henry Wieman, use the God word to describe the larger naturalistic reality of the cosmos at work. (See Patton's *Redefining Religion*, pp. 2–5; "creativity" is Wieman's emphasis).

Kenneth avoided any confusion about his belief in a naturalistic materialism without supernatural intervention. He wants to be clear that his religious humanism comes from an agnostic and even atheistic position. (Hence the title of his book in 1982, *A Happy Atheist*.)

Patton carries the Emerson revolution of a naturalistic mysticism or spiritual experiencing even further by avoiding in most cases the traditional religious language and clearly saying that this world-cosmos and everything in it is *the* reality—that humans and their fundamental principles are the arena for our ongoing religious work—that we are intimately interconnected, as is every atom with every other person—and that there is a powerful realization of this out of the mystical experiences and religious knowledge we gain from these prime connections.

He goes on to define these fundamental universal principles, operative for all people, all interwoven like a wire cable stranded together.

> The first is a principle of humanity that assumes the selfhood, worth, dignity, and reality of persons.
>
> 2nd. The principle of life—that we "treasure life" and are "guardians of life."
>
> 3rd. That there is a simplicity to wisdom "centering in on a few principles— this life, subject to splintering, knots into unity."
>
> 4th. The principle of non-violence.
>
> 5th. The principle of self-possession—that "we possess ourselves and no creature has any right over us."
>
> 6th. The principle of nurture—that "the processes of Nature will sustain us if we use them rightly." (*Redefining Religion*, Meeting House Press)

It is here that we find Kenneth wavering between the poles of a dialectic that have typified the humanist perspective. On the one hand there is the notion that the universe is neutral to us, does not care for or nurture us, that it "treats us like the sacrificial straw dogs," as LaoTze says, tossing us onto the edge of the road when the ritual celebration is over. Kenneth talks about "the blind dark unknowingness of the galactic space, insensible to our existence"—"The working of the world is terrible with unconcern" (*Man Is the Meaning*, p. 46). Then his mystical experience comes to bear—speaking of the inter-connection of one atom to another—our body to the galactic body—a unity of existence.

On the other hand there is the notion of the singular, self-possessed, unique being of each one of us. He writes:

> "Every creature is alone in its life process; an involuntary, inevitable outworking." (*Religion of Realities*, p. 1)

Contrast this with:

> "We have been kin for billions of years in this common home, in one family of life." (*Ibid.*, p. 146)

Furthermore:

> "Our senses have revealed the world to us, and enabled us to survive in it." (*Ibid,* p. 148)

Like Freud, Patton believes that our senses have developed in touch with the world about us, as a hand fits a glove, giving us intimate knowledge of the world, allowing us to survive.

Is the universe blind and uncaring; are we singular and alone?—as one pole of his thinking would have it. Or in fact is our intuitive mystical knowledge of our kinship and connection and the caring nurturance of the cosmos for our life and the life process not the truer, religious insight?

Kenneth Patton's religious philosophy did not grow out of any mainly academic or philosophical tradition. It took shape in the context of an experimental religious congregation with a mission to create a new expression for Universalism in the mid-twentieth century. His creative work was taking place in a developing congregation in the midst of Boston, a large city. Thus it did not have an ethereal or esoteric quality, but rather was tailored to people's needs and expressed often in poetic religious language.

He made two particular contributions to midcentury Universalism: (1) He believed in and set up a structure allowing democratic participation and dialogue in shaping our contemporary faith, and (2) he made an effort to create a universal religion out of the whole human heritage.

Patton believed that a democratic process of dialogue is essential for the development of a universalist faith. He opened up the worship setting into the round, and gave room for dialogue with the minister as part of the process of exchange of the word. Though Kenneth could be dogmatic and difficult, freedom of expression was encouraged, and the worship service was opened up into a more sharing and less authoritarian structure for presentation.

No one of that era contributed more concretely to the expansion of Universalism from a Judeo-Christian-based literature and liturgy toward a wide-open, inclusive embrace of the world's culture and arts—the complete range of the religious heritage of humankind. He tracked down and introduced religious literature, both contemporary and ancient, from all culture, Sunday worship services.

As an example: He was deeply influenced by the kinship of his own natural mysticism with that same heritage from China in the writings of the Taoists and neo-Confucianists. In particular, he utilized Feng Yu-lan, a great twentieth-Century Chinese philosopher who had written a 2-volume work called *The Spirit of Chinese Philosophy*, which is a classic standard.

Kenneth took Feng's delineation of four spheres of our human religious life and built services around Feng's concepts:

- The Sphere of Innocence—the development and responsibility for self-hood.
- The Sphere of Utility—work and survival in life.
- The Sphere of Morality.
- The Sphere of Transcendence—the upward turning for meaning and hope.

He then used readings from Feng and his own amplification of these themes, together with recorded Chinese music and works from the art collection of the Meeting House that had been collected to illustrate world religious cultures. This was a carrying forward creatively and ritualistically of the groundbreaking publishing by Emerson and Thoreau of world religious writings in *The Dial* a century before.

There were times when the Meeting House and its creative experiments in contemporary worship seemed a little arty and eclectic. However, the services Patton and his congregation created never failed to stimulate and open up the experience of the human religious spirit past and present—and to make clear that we were in a large, diverse world that shared universal hopes and perspectives, a one-human religious heritage of depth and challenging worth.

Kenneth Patton saw a necessary connection between a universal religion for one world and the bringing about necessary world government of the United Nations for the nurturance and preservation of peace and common wealth in the world. Instead of the kingdom of God as the vision of the world to be realized, Patton envisioned the creation of true community and a common wealth to be shared equitably among all people.

"Salvation," he writes, "is to be that goodness our persons can accomplish" (*Religion of Realities*, p. 43). "Social responsibility inheres in the indivisible social world from which we all receive sustenance, imposing its obligations on all who are sensitive to humane appeals" (*Ibid.*, p. 191).

Although social activism was not one of Kenneth's strong suits, he spoke out fearlessly for a "social vision" from his pulpit at a time when "anticommunism" was a theme to ride for a successful political career. He was bold enough to open his church for the free assembly of the Communist Party USA when all halls were closed to them in Boston. The Charles Street Meeting House remained a free and open arena for the broadest free expression of all points of view.

This inadequate overview of Kenneth Patton's religious philosophy is meant to only touch on some of the significant perspectives that reveal his real contribution to Unitarian Universalism and American religious life. He was far from systematic in his philosophy, yet very few preachers made such a self-conscious or sustained effort to redefine and develop an overall liberal religious agenda.

His truly significant contribution was not any particular idea *de novo* but his bringing to bear a poetic, mystical intelligence that presented a fresh new approach for worship presentation in nontraditional humanistic language and naturalistic religious philosophy. This, at a time when older liberal Christian expression was effete, empty, nonbelievable. It was plainly not relevant to a newly emerging, scientifically educated American generation that wanted a religious life of the spirit that befitted and jibed with the new educated consciousness they were entering. Patton provided an articulate, coherent, and crafted religious context for many in our Unitarian Universalist movement. His contribution must not be undervalued, despite his shortcomings and the faddish trends of today.

Because his most lasting gift will be some of his outstanding poetry crafted for religious services, I end with one of my favorites.

At-Homeness

Gather into yourself all of the world.
    Lie on the earth and feast on the sky.
Print upon the films of your eyes' inner theatre the
images of all its forms and creatures.
Record upon your inner ear the sounds of water and
wind, leaves and birds, the voices and songs of people.
Gather the stars into your mind, and the knowledge of
huge spaces and the length of time.
    Be rich with friends and companions.
Discover the loveliness of your mate and your fortune in
the faces and hands of your children.
Give and be given unto, that within you may be stored
and reborn all of the world about you.
You, who are nature, be all of nature;

For nothing can be strange to you, and never in the
heavens and earth can you be homeless.

Chapter 12

The Road Not Taken:
A Critical Response to
A Religion for One World:
Art and Symbols for a Universal Religion
(Kenneth L. Patton, Boston, Beacon Press and
Meeting House Press, 1964)

Thomas R. Schade

Imagining a new religion is no easy task, especially one that is universal, or at least seeks a universal appeal. Consequently, evaluating someone else's efforts at such a task is even more difficult. Naturally, I feel constrained in my comments by the fact that I myself have never put my hand to starting even a smallish cult. I doubt my ability here as much as I doubt my qualifications to to judge another's form at tight rope walking or their skill at childbirth.

I am further constrained in evaluating Patton's work by this fact. On page 3 of *A Religion for One World,* he says, "The major argument within the Association centers on whether Unitarian Universalism shall be a world religion or the liberal wing of Protestant Christianity." His book is a document of the journey on the former path. I myself would prefer the road not taken, that Unitarian Universalists had made a steady and persistent effort since our merger to speak to the ever more evident facts of one world, one humanity, one future, from within our historic position on the far liberal edge of Protestantism. So please forgive me if I occasionally wax acidic, even bilious, as I try to make sense of the Charles Street Meeting House. I find myself in the unhappy position of trying to evaluate work that not only have I never tried but that I would not have ever tried, and that I don't think should have even been tried. The reader should be warned that just thinking about the Charles Meeting House often puts me in a bad mood.

Further, I cannot really evaluate the historic significance of the Charles Street Meeting House project. I don't have a firm enough grasp of what else was going in the Association at that time. Were the ideas expressed by Patton novel and brilliant, and significant because they were ground-breaking? Or did he grab the zeitgeist and brilliantly reflect what was going around? I don't know. I was in high school in 1964, in the Liberal Religious Youth (LRY) group of the First Unitarian Church in Youngstown, Ohio, trying to acquire a taste for Bob Dylan's singing voice and Marlboro cigarettes. The Rev. Frank Schulman was our minister, and our church was unmistakably a part of liberal Protestantism. If I shared any of Ken Patton's concerns at the time, it went no further than my bemused wondering why it was that, in the church, what was clearly a *lobby* was called a *narthex*.

Overview

The Charles Street Meeting House project seems the result of humanism seeking a positive encounter with all the world religions. The motivation seems largely the desire to negate Christianity as much as possible. Patton wants to get as far as possible from the dogmatic certainty of the church—of its claim to be a divine revelation—through a commitment to science and experiment. The encounter with world religions is more complicated. He wants to transcend the division of the world into competing religions and begin the process of building a universal religion. There is an inherent contradiction between an affirmation of world religions and building a new universal religion, even in prototype. If all the world religions are just fine, then why do we need a new one, especially one that proposes universality? So any proposal must be able to explain its theology of religions: an explanation of the origin of religious variety in the world; a method for comparing them, determining their differences and similarities, and evaluating them.

Further, the desire to build a universal religion places Patton squarely in the mainstream of Christian history, which has also been about building a universal religion. This, of course, is exactly where Patton does not want to be, so one of the challenges he faces is developing a social strategy for establishing the new religion without engaging in conversion efforts.

The Religion for One World Is Humanism

Make no mistake about this central fact: the theological and philosophical underpinning of the entire Charles Street Meeting House experiment was humanism. "[I]t is my conviction that any experiment toward a religion for one world must be thoroughly naturalistic and scientific in its approach to what it will tentatively believe about the human situation." [8]

Every other kind of religious knowledge, according to Patton, is distorted by the language of its particular historical culture. Moreover, those who do not share its cultural framework will find it unpalatable. Science, however, is a process capable of determining truth from material reality independent of culture. But Patton has a further insight. Scientific naturalism not only challenges what is supernatural and superstitious in all religion and all culture, but it has also revealed the information that is the basis of a new religious consciousness. The *Religion for One World* is precisely that—a religion that seeks to base itself on the insight that modern science has put before us: humanity is one species arising out of one evolutionary process, on one planet, and shares one fate. It is not only a religion for one world; it is the religion about one world.

Some of the symbols, the art, and the design for the Meeting House reflected this purpose. The mural of the Andromeda Nebula and the sculpture of the atom were designed to create awe and wonder by representing the scientific truth now known. Symbolically, they are synecdoche; they convey the whole by showing a part. They are not metaphorical, in that they attempt to show the part realistically and accurately. They are iconic—windows into reality, not just images of reality. They are designed to show the scale of the universe so powerfully that they force a change in one's cosmology. They show the breadth of human knowledge. "Look," they say, "from the largest scale to the smallest scale, human beings can show the very structure of the Universe." (The veiled subtext is also that as we have looked from the tiniest scale to the grandest scale, we still can't see any sign of God.) They have the power of the later images of the Earth taken by astronauts returning from the moon: never before seen pictures of what reality really is. To some degree, they have lost their power now through repetition, but they also could force a change in one's understanding of humanity. Seen from the moon, the divisions among the Earth's people into nations, races, religions, and peoples of many types, seem pointless and retrograde.

The modem scientific worldview also seemed to have a major influence on the art and design of the Meeting House project in that it negates all forms of established authority in favor of free dialogue, open questioning, and the equality of persons. Hence the commitment to experimentalism in method. And hence some of the other design elements of the Charles Street Meeting House experiment: the open hymnals, the congregation in the round, the minister on the same level as the congregation, the discussion period following the sermon.

It is these proposals, because they are based on an understanding of the social implications of the scientific method, that have a profoundly antitraditional character in religion. Science stands opposed to any practice or authority that is legitimated only by tradition or history. The volume before us (*A Religion for One World*) offers theoretical justifications for liturgical practices that became standard fare in most Unitarian Universalist churches. Patton makes it clear that the origins of most of our ultra-democratic liturgical practices lie in an appropriation of some of the spirit of science by worship.

Of course, some would argue that to apply the norms of public scientific discourse to the practice of worship is like using Occam's razor to change a baby's diaper. If a researcher states a conclusion in public discussion about his topic, he or she should be prepared to defend it against critical inquiry from any individual present. Should a minister who states in a sermon a long-held teaching of the religious tradition (for example, that God loves humanity, individually as well as in a group) be subject to the same scrutiny? Perhaps there is a soul in attendance who needs to hear this unproven assertion anyway. Is a worship service ultimately about searching for verifiable truth? And if the worship service is not about verifiable truths, then what is the effect of using the norms of open inquiry and free criticism in evaluating the service? The unwillingness of science to defer to past authority results in an ever-advancing pursuit of the truth. The unwillingness of a congregation to defer to any external authority, especially in the form of a minister speaking from the accumulated wisdom of a religious tradition, can result in an ever-narrower worship defined by the comfort level of the congregation.

The Theology of Religions of the Charles Street Meeting House Project

> We identify, not with the particular theology, magic or ritual practice, but rather with the prevailing hunger and searching that led . . . people through whatever means to seek answers to their questions [and to seek to] produce, security, beauty and hope. . . . [N]o matter how superstitious, unenlightened, unscientific, even brutal the religious practice may seem to be, the intent, the drive behind the religious practice is something which we share and in which we can have full identity and participation. (*RFOW*, p. 12)

The belief that there exists a universal religious impulse everywhere among humanity, the universal natural religion, became the true meaning of Universalism, as opposed to its original identity as the Christian doctrine of universal salvation.

Humanity's religions are understood primarily from an anthropological perspective. It believes that there is, within humanity, a universal religious drive behind all cult and theology. Patton quotes A. Eustace Haydon: "It is man's [sic] search through the changing ages for the values that may make our common earthly life glad and beautiful and good."

Should we be surprised that such a formulation happens to match almost exactly the modem secularist understanding of the finer things of life? Of course not. Most efforts to discern the essence of humanity end up in some form of projection on the part of the searcher. I question whether this very humble modern desire to know what makes life glad, beautiful, and good was the motivation of the Buddha, of the Apostle Paul, of Confucius, of the Prophet Mohammed, of Augustine of Hippo, of George Fox and of Mary Baker Eddy, and countless others. Certainly many of them would not recognize Haydon's formulation as representing their deepest concerns.

The ambition of the Charles Street Meeting House project, however, derived from the belief that if you could distill the entire religious history of humanity, removing every impurity, every trace element picked up from the surrounding soil, the end product, the clear pure liquid left at the end, would be scientific naturalism. The *A Religion For One World* is not the refutation of all previous world religions; it is their completion and perfection.

This constitutes a different relationship between world religion and humanism than had been envisioned earlier. Apparently the earlier humanists thought all world religions were obstacles to the real truth. Superstitious, filled with supernatural and miraculous elements, religion was one way that magical thinking held humanity in thrall. Humanism was to religion as truth is to falsehood. The religion for the one world is to religion as pure is to impure, or as Danish Modern is to Victorian.

Kenneth Patton was not a pluralist according to our current categories of the interreligious encounter. Patton is an inclusivist, one who believes other religions to be imperfect and inferior manifestations of his own, the one true religion.

Further, it is exactly the cultural specificity of all the other religions that makes them inferior to the religion for one world. In order to be convinced of the truth of any religion, the potential convert has to learn the ways of the culture from which that religion springs. In order to understand Christianity, one has to be able to decode all those references to Israel and Judea and Galilee and grasp the history of Rome and Europe. To make any sense of Hinduism, one has to learn an enormous amount of information about the Indian subcontinent, its history, and its culture. It is their cultural specificity that makes them unlikely to become a universal religion.

Hence the use of the symbols and sacred texts of other religious traditions has a curiously ironic feel in the descriptions of the Charles Street Meeting House. The Meeting House contained an impressive collection of the religious symbols and artwork from around the world and annals of history. But these, of course, are held at an emotional distance. They are interesting because they document the imperfect expression of the true hidden natural religion in human history. They document steps on the journey, but not the end of it.

The mural of the Andromeda Nebula is powerful because it conveys a powerful truth to us, in our time. A painting of the Buddha, or an African mask, is intriguing, or curious, or fascinating, because it once had the same effect on another person that the galaxy mural has on us.

The Potential Social Base of the Religion of One World

The religion for one world is not likely to be celebrated at the church around the comer unless you live around the comer from the United Nations. Only those who have transreligious experience and have been disillusioned by the narrow superstition of their own religious heritage will see the need for the religion for one world. The religion for one world is not envisioned as a community of devout Hindus, Buddhists, Christians, and Muslims. It is envisioned as a community of disillusioned Hindus, Buddhists, Christians, and Muslims. For many decades and centuries it will be able to appeal only to that highly educated, well-traveled, cosmopolitan class which makes up a particular political, social, and intellectual elite. The pace of development of this religious tendency would be dependent on the pace of the development of a world citizenry, a class of people with enough experience through increased communications and transportation to be able to make relative their own tradition.

The process of leaving one's cultural traditions behind to become a global citizen is at the heart of the conversion experience to the religion for one world.

Patton sees this as being his own story:

> As a child, I was a Methodist. When, after 15 years of slow evolution, I ceased to be a Christian, I was not then disposed to join some other movement, to be a Jew, a Moslem, a Hindu or a Buddhist. I belonged to no tradition in the old sense. I had left my cultural provincialism and "belonging" behind, even as I had left behind the "upper-lower class" into which I was born. I believe that I am now free from both social-class and denominational parochialism. Nothing will satisfy me short of being a member of the human race and having a religion for one world. (p. 17, *RFOW*).

Since 1964

The Charles Street Meeting House was based on three interlocking ideas:

1. An anthropological understanding of humanity's religions, each an imperfect and culturally bound manifestation of a natural and universal religious impulse,
2. Scientific naturalism as a pure and culturally neutral expression of the universal religion,
3. The conversion of the world's people to scientific naturalism, beginning with the elites, who would be first disenchanted with

the imperfections of their religious roots and then attracted by the truth of scientific naturalism, if it were presented well.

Each idea has gone through an important reexamination since the Patton book was published. The ideas are still around, but modified, and recombined in a new way. Because each idea was connected to the other, it is hard to trace historically in what order these ideas fell, but each did.

The first question that arises is whether there is, in fact, a universal impulse towards religion present in every age and culture. We do know that human beings seem to have a religious impulse as a sort of cultural universal. But are all of those urges directed to the same ends, and do they represent the same relationship to the universe?

We really have no idea and there may be no way to really find out. Is there any way that someone can really understand another's religious thinking—from the inside out? When we hear of someone else's religious feelings, and they seem similar to our own, are we accurately hearing that person without projecting our own religious feelings as theirs?

So why reduce the wide variety of world religious expression to variations on a single unheard theme? Isn't it simply sufficient to accept the vast diversity of religious expression on its own terms? Can't we just celebrate the differences rather than trying to draw everything together into a unity?

But there is a purpose to the belief that all religions arise out of the same human impulse. Such belief preserves a hierarchy of religions. Once an ideal type is identified, some religions, and some people, will be seen as closer to the ideal than others. Islam, it appears, is much further from the ideal than is Buddhism. But closest of all, apparently, is Unitarian Universalism, at least in its natural mystic mode.

Of all the ideas that were current in the early 1960s, none has been more decisively refuted in the last 40 years than the thought that the North American middle class was somehow closer to the universal human experience than any other group. Other people were thought to see reality through the filter of their culture, but we saw life as it really was. Our worldview was thought to be universal. But this refuted idea is central to the religion for one world. But now we have come to know that the ways of thinking, living, and worshipping among us are as culturally and historically distinctive as those of any aboriginal band's in the Australian outback, or those of the typical small peasant village in Peru, or those of an average worker's neighborhood in Central Europe.

The second change is that humanism is now no longer considered to be the final destination of all religious thinking. At one point, humanists thought that as scientific knowledge grew, the pull of religion would weaken. Once the supernatural elements were rejected by thinking people, then the religions could converge on the basis of the celebration of objective truth. Yet science advances continuously, and religions continue to have power. Human beings rely on a scientific and technical worldview to negotiate their way through the everyday, while at the same time holding religious opinions which cannot be supported by any sort of factual analysis. What was an irreconcilable problem for European and North American intellectuals in the nineteenth and twentieth centuries appears not to be that big a deal for much of the rest of the world.

Religious liberals now mutter darkly about the rising tide of fundamentalism. We should remember, however, that even within the Unitarian Universalist Association, it is religion that has made relative scientific humanism, not the other way around. Scientific humanism is now considered to be just one religious tendency among many possible among religious liberals. Only a few choose to make it the standard by which they judge their religious opinions. Humanism has lost its privileged place as the gatekeeper to the UU temple, keeping out fuzzy thinking and irrational enthusiasm. It now must coexist with other religious tendencies.

History has not treated Patton's predictions of the social base of the religion for one world with any more kindness. His prediction was that the process of what we now call "globalization" would result in a growing class of people who were disillusioned by the narrowness of their religious tradition. In other words, the experience of religious liberals leaving Christianity was going to be repeated everywhere. Islam would create religious liberals, as would Shintoism, as would African animism. And all these religious liberals would find each other and make congregations.

Of all the claims that are made in the volume, perhaps the most dated seem to be Kenneth Patton's claims that the midcentury North

American humanist has been able to transcend the particularities of time and place and culture and attain a universal consciousness.

Most external observers would doubt that Kenneth Patton had actually transcended his cultural, national, and religious roots, even though they may have been causing him great pain and embarrassment. It would be not for the lack of trying. It is just that it can't be done. Culture and history are cumulative; nothing is ever "left behind." Kenneth Patton may have wanted to leave Christianity and the marks of an "upper-lower" class background behind. He was an attempted former Christian. He was a disaffected Christian and did important religious work as a naturalistic mystical, poetic, and ecstatic disaffected Christian. He was an important leader of a religious movement composed of many other attempted former Christians. But most of his work was an extended struggle and dialogue with Christianity.

The point is not the ineffectiveness of Patton's attempted escape from Christianity. The point is that the religion for one world's proposed social base was to be lots of people just like Kenneth Patton. This was, of course, not to be. If there were people who did have the same relationship to Islam, Buddhism, to Sikhism, to paganism as Patton had (and most UU's have) toward Christianity, they probably congregated each among themselves. It does not seem that they sought common worship and congregational life with disaffected Christians in any great number.

It is ironic, of course, that Christianity, for all of its cultural embeddedness, has been far more able to transcend the limits of its cultural roots and become global than has any version of Boston-based Unitarian Universalism. There are more Christians in Africa than in Europe as we enter the third millennium. Islam, as well, has been remarkably successful in many different cultural settings.

Is the Road Ahead the Road Not Taken?

Kenneth Patton proposed that Unitarian Universalism commit itself to becoming a new world religion, making a clean break with liberal Protestantism. And this has been, for the most part, the road that the

Association has taken, although not always following the example of the Charles Street Meeting House. However, since then, the theological underpinnings to our claim of being a new world religion have come undone. We are like the cartoon character whose legs are moving but who has run off the cliff. The problem that we now face is this: We are no longer willing to claim that our version of naturalistic mysticism (humanism) is the purest expression of the essence of all other religions. We now admit that it is just another take on religion, one that comes out of our particular history and social location. The meaning of the word universalism has shifted again, away from an ambition to embody an ideal universal religion, toward a willingness to accept the universal validity of all religions in their particularity. We no longer see ourselves as proposing the solution to the problem of the complex relationships of competition and cooperation between the great variety of world religions, because we no longer see them as a problem.

But when we give up the effort to be the solution to a nonexistent problem, we also give up the reason why we felt it necessary to cut ourselves off from our real roots in liberal congregationally-based Protestantism. If we now know that we are unable to transcend our historical particularity, and if we now know that our religious views are no closer to the "natural religion," then shouldn't we claim our authentic selves as liberal Protestants?

Every problem that Kenneth Patton saw with Christianity was and is a real problem. Its focus on right belief has resulted in dogmatism and intellectual authoritarianism. It has historically made exclusivist claims and adopted an arrogant view of nonbelievers. Its roots in ancient history and culture mean that it is filled with myth, magic, and unscientific thinking. Its understandings of revelation and inspiration are an epistemological quagmire. All this and more: celebration of patriarchy, homophobia, compromises with power and wealth. None of this can be denied, and Christianity needs Christians who are not in denial. We inherited a 2,000-year-old house, and most things that are that old need a lot of repair.

We know all that. What we did not know, in the heady days of the merger, was that we were among the ones chosen by history and circumstance to struggle on behalf of the truths we know within the Christian tradition. We walked away from that task to pursue another road, one that has led into a self-contained cul-de-sac.

It is time to face the facts of who we are, and of what is needed in this culture, and take the road not taken, the only road that connects our past with our future.

Section IV

Last Things

Chapter 13

Meeting House Symbols at Starr King School for the Ministry

Alicia McNary Forsey

A substantial number of the symbols which were originally made and used at the Charles Street Universalist Meeting House now have an honored home at Starr King School for the Ministry in Berkeley, California. It is my understanding that they became available to the seminary when the Meeting House was shut down.

Paul Sawyer, now minister of the Throop Memorial UU Church in Pasadena, California, was then in Boston. He found that he could purchase them for the school—his Alma Mater—for a small sum. Then-President Richard Kimball agreed to pay the amount requested. Paul then brought them to the West Coast along with some objects from the art collection of the Meeting House.

The symbols are displayed in the rafters of the main room at the seminary, the Fireplace Room, a warm and beautiful space at the heart of the school. They have been there for a long time, as I remember them during the time that I was a student, in 1973–1976, though I do not remember anybody explaining their history or meaning to me.

These days, every new class that begins at Starr King School has a week of orientation. I have a couple of hours each year to relate the basic history of the school and to identify the treasures one may find within it. I always speak about the symbols from the Charles Street Meeting House. I am mindful of them because, aside from them being in the rafters directly over my head as I speak, they are quite unique and come from the Universalist side of our tradition, which is always given the short end of the stick as far as having our attention. Also, there is a display consisting of small photos of the symbols, with an explanation of the significance of each one, in the room where the symbols are mounted. So a student or a guest may consult the guide in order to get a better understanding of a specific symbol.

The students are clearly attached to the symbols. There have been two "work parties" focused on cleaning all of the symbols within the last few years. Students bring their friends and family to see the symbols. I frequently hear them relating the history of the symbols to someone who is not familiar with them. I think there is a feeling that we have "rescued" something of great value.

Now and then a student will check one out in order to take it with her or him to deliver a Universalist sermon. I understand that Ken Patton was not completely accepted by many of his Universalist colleagues, but I have never tried to stop students from identifying with him as a Universalist because of this. Patton had a different notion about Universalism, probably one that is more compatible with the thinking of students today than the Universalism of many ministers in New England who opposed him.

I do discuss with my students the Consolidation of 1961, and ask them to consider what the theology, the governance, and the resources were for each tradition. I inevitably get hard questions relating to how decisions were made to close the seminaries, why the Charles Street Meeting House was sold and so on. I know that when I go to visit Boston, it saddens me deeply to walk by what was once the Charles Street Meeting House. Now it is a complex of offices and shops. The bed and breakfast where I sometimes stay (Pickett/Eliot House on Beacon Hill) is owned by the Unitarian Universalist Association. There is a map in each room of all the Unitarian and Universalist churches in town—those that have been closed and those that remain open.

So many have been closed and sold. I have to wonder why the UUA did not keep the Meeting House property and make the building useful. Things change, but that is all the more reason to keep our roots planted.

Chapter 14

The Future of Universalism

Kenneth L. Patton

(Address delivered to the 157th annual session of the New York State Convention of Universalists, Oneonta, New York, October 19, 1985)

My liberal religion was developed within the Protestant tradition, culminating at the Divinity School at the University of Chicago, under teachers who were also Protestants, but whose beliefs had developed into religious humanism, naturalism, and a "science of religion." It was a movement quite independent of Unitarianism and Universalism. I became a Unitarian because it allowed me to expound and develop my religious humanism. I had already left their original heresies, the unity of God and universal salvation, far behind. Since I no longer believed in God, it was small concern whether he was three or one or one thousand. Since I no longer believed in salvation, or any existence after death, whether there was both a heaven and a hell, or just a heaven, was an idle quandary. Thus my present opinion is the same as when I came into lib-eral religion 43 years ago: that in its original formulation, Universalism has no future at all; it is an outworn fantasy.

When I shifted from Unitarian to Universalist ranks seven years later, and moved to Boston, I discovered that Universalism was a progressive, evolving idea. The word universal was a great word, with a multitude of creative applications. Under Clarence Skinner, head of the Tufts School of Religion and the Community Church in Boston, Universalism was now related to universal peace, justice, equality, to one world, one humanity. I launched a creative program at the Charles Street Meeting House to explore the possibilities of a religion for one world. We created a laboratory model of such a religion through a dozen integrated projects. But it was not simply that, for it was also the living religion of the people of the Meeting House. I believe we succeeded in our experiment. But we failed in the sense that other liberal societies did not make it a model for their reconstruction. Oh, it had various influences and partial imitations. But our now merged association has not become universal in the sense we demonstrated. The Meeting House is gone, its collections of art, symbols, world bibles, music vandalized and dispersed, the building sold to an architectural organization. The temple of Universalism we created has been demolished and now exists only in the book that described the process and philosophy of its creation.

When we ask about the future of Universalism, we are in fact asking two questions: Frist, what is the future of Universalism within the Unitarian Universalist Association? Second, what is the future of universalism in the world at large? And between these two questions there is a very important issue. In supernatural and theistic religions, their ultimate success is guaranteed in a life and world beyond this, a process magnificently and hugely projected in Michelangelo's great mural on the last judgment. In Islam the faithful will graduate at death into paradise. The future of Hinduism is reincarnation, and ultimately release from the wheel of rebirth, and in Buddhism it is nirvana.

But the future of a natural and human religion of universalism is an entirely different matter. It is a religion of human achievements and relationships in this world, here and now. It is entirely dependent on human character and achievements, on human behavior, and dependent on the environment of planet earth. We are subject to earthquakes, volcanic eruptions, hurricanes, tornadoes, to desertification, drought, and our own pollution and depredations, to war, hatred, and greed. Given the unreliability of the earth itself, and our own waywardness, the success of this idealistic universal religion is far from assured. That is, we have no assurance that our own denomination will become truly universal, and we have no assurance that humanity as a whole will become universal. We have no assurance that we will survive the nuclear crisis. Lewis Thomas has stated the issue perfectly: What we need most of all is a future.

If we created an adequate universalist religion of our own, what would we have? I have spent my professional life proving out a conviction: that this universal religion is "out there," in human history, in art, literature, philosophy, in science, archaeology, anthropology, paleontology, in history. And it is there. One of the projects in Boston, our "open hymnal," has been continued, and is now culminated in the publishing of four *Hymns of Humanity* volumes. A life of research has produced 1100 song verses of high literary quality, and thousands of pieces of poetry and prose for readings. Twenty-five years ago it provided some eighty hymns and ninety readings for *Hymns for the Celebration of Life*. Some forty of those hymns found their way into the new English Unitarian hymn book.

Our problem lies in the discrepancy between what is available to us and what we make use of. Take a specific instance: Frank Lloyd Wright was born a Unitarian, his father and uncle were leaders in liberal religion. Perhaps the greatest architect ever born was one of us. But in a long lifetime he built one Universalist and one Unitarian Church building. We could have had a hundred Wright buildings across the land. There is a wealth of art and symbolism available to us, but most of our temples are barren of both. We have a treasury of great literature expressing our free, natural, and human faith. Our next hymn book could be a literary treasury. We will probably use but a fraction of it because of our reluctance to give up our denominational doggerel. The great poets have written for us. The great painters and sculptors have wrought for us. The great architects would serve us. Music, dance, and drama wait for our adoption.

In order to make use of the treasures that are ours for the taking, we have to escape the narrowness and provincialism of our own past. Granted that our roots were in the Judeo-Christian tradition, but do we have to be stuck in the rut in which we originated? The first axiom of a universal religion is that it is world-wide, and humanity-wide. It so happens that our history is mainly in China and not in the West. Our religion is 3,000 years old in China, where the greatest philosophers, poets, and painters created Chinese naturalism, humanism, and universalism. But do we have the wits, taste, acumen, scholarship, and appreciation to avail ourselves of this magnificent cultural treasure? I call it our "Chinese connection," and I have published four books on it. Our roots also go into the Old Stone Age, where humanity had no gods, but related to the earth, the wind, and the sun and stars, and was in profound collaboration with the earth and its other creatures. I have just published its major storehouse, *Kaggen, the Mantis.* I do not say this by way of self-glorification. I have simply explored and practiced my own religion, my universalism, during this one brief life given us. I could not have used this life to better purpose, with greater personal rewards of fundamen-tal satisfactions.

What is the future of Universalism as the religion of some 200,000 UUs? The answer is paradoxical: We have a magnificent universalist religion, which we largely ignore and make no use of. Its fact is not in the future. It is here now. What is in the future is whether we will become aware of the great religion that is available to us, that is "out there," and bring it "in here," and make it our own. Are we big enough, intelligent enough, appreciative enough, wise enough, to acclaim that universal religion that already exists, awaiting our espousal?

But the paradox is of even more vast dimensions. Say that we did accomplish all this: What would it amount to? The experiments in Boston not only involved the collection, the designs, the interpretations. They involved our personal reactions to them, as members of a parish, as members of a Universalist Society. We were our own guinea pigs. Did this work for us, on a weekday level, from Sunday to Sunday? After one of our festival services, a visitor was heard to remark: "These people really believe this." And we did. We had our universal religion, even as we labored to create it. What if all 200,000 of us had this universal religion? What would it amount to? What effect would it have on the world, on the hope and fate of humanity? Probably not much: 200,000 in 240 million is not a considerable percentage. In some five billions of human beings planet-wide, even less. Three thousand years of Chinese humanism has not transfigured the human family. Such a religion would greatly enrich our societies and our personal lives. This is our major consideration, the enrichment of our family and personal lives, of the religious fellowship. We cannot wait until the world endorses our universal religion. We must celebrate and live it now, and make it meaningful to our children. In an amusing sense, universalism becomes a parochial matter, a fellowship concern. It is also a personal matter, for it permeates the reveries, the meditations, and the sensibility of each of us. It is the aura, the atmosphere of the day. It is a profoundly intimate and private matter, even as it ramifies out into the entire human family, the planet, even the universe. We are creatures, not just of planet earth, but of the whole, blooming universe, in which our planet and its stars are tiny, but native, denizens.

In a sense, even denominationally, the future of Universalism is a personal matter. Ultimately, each of us is responsible for the fullness of a universal religious experience that is our own, our personal religion. I must confess to a profound pessimism as to the likelihood that our own Unitarian Universalist Association will realize the future of the universalist religion that is available to it. My disrespect for denominational bureaucracy, organization, politics, "leadership," professionalism, is profound. I have virtually no respect for denominational, organizational religion. I do not believe it should be called religion at all. Religion in any real sense is what happens in the individual, in the personal idealism, dreams, hunger, sorrow, and aspiration of the person. Denominations are the dry, dead branches, the debris of living religion.

What is the future of universal religion? You will answer that in the privacy of your own person. Each of us has a personal love affair with reality, with the universe. I have expressed it thus:

> One blossom on my tulip tree,
> fresh opened, first day in the sun,
> first day in air, a white delight,
> its scent a frail delirium:
>
> It is all blossoms of the world,
> all flowers since world of flowers began,

that triumph of the universe
that made it flower, that made me man.

To me that is all that religion, in its reality, amounts to, the zest, the creativity, the belongingness that permeates the private life of the individual. That is the only reality religion has.

This matter of the future of universalism has for me, a personal irony. It is in religion that universalism should have its fullest, its most profound expression. And yet religion is congenitally averse to affirming and espousing universalism. It is perennially parochial, local, tribal. Religion protests that it espouses universal love, forgiveness, charity, yet it practices the meanest hatred, rancor, niggardliness, and vengeance. Judaism is torn between the love of God and the wrath of God. The irony is that universalism fails as the ideal of religion but succeeds as the ideal of dozens of secular, academic, artistic, cultural agencies. A news item from last week: "Academics and political leaders gathered to pay tribute to Edwin 0. Reischauer, America's foremost expert on Japan, and to celebrate the opening of the new Reischauer Center of East Asian Studies at the Johns Hopkins University School of Advanced International Studies. . . . Mr. Reischauer told the audience that his life aim in 1931 was to draw attention to Asia. 'Today, the field has grown far beyond anything I dreamed of,' he said. 'This ambition has been more than fulfilled.'"

The future of universalism, in the broader perspective, is assured, because universalism is factual, realistic. The root of the word is "universe." There is but one "universe." If this is true, universalism is the only future the human race has. If it is not true, then a hornet's nest of rancorous and bestial animosities has been loosed. If the fundamentalists are right, there is only one piece of advice: find a place to hide.

The theme of the future of universalism is being played out not in religious societies, but in universities, in museums, in cultural agencies. My observations inevitably have a personal referrant.

In the Meeting House in Boston we created centers of world religions and cultures. Each had its essential art objects and symbols. All that is gone. But in the Brooklyn Museum of Art all of those centers are intact, and their art magnificently displayed. At the Metropolitan Museum of Art, the process goes on unrelentingly, to show that art and culture are universal. Primitive and tribal art, Chinese art, Japanese art, Hindu art, Near Eastern art, Grecian and Roman art, all areas have been widened and deepened. Culture and art are universal. A true museum of art is a museum of world art, a museum of universal human culture.

Religion has no monopoly on religion. Universities and museums can be far more realistic and idealistic than religious denominations. In Kansas City I was speaking on universal religion. Two blocks away was one of the world's great assemblages of Chinese naturalistic and humanistic arts. Several times I walked over to share it. The Unitarians and Universalists of the area knew nothing of the riches they harbored. Museums and universities go on about their business, regardless of the quandaries of religious bureaucracies. Reality is reality. It has nothing to do with denominations, boards, public relations strategies.

The collection of the art of the world's religions we assembled in Boston had been dispersed. But the museums have become truly universal. The centers of World culture exist in the Brooklyn Museum in almost the same form we gave them in the Meeting House. The Metropolitan is possibly the most dramatic example, with superlative collections of primitive and tribal art, Near Eastern and Islamic Art, the art of Egypt, Greece and Rome, Christian art, a new Chinese gallery, and new galleries of Japanese and Hindu and South Asian art in preparation. It is now a museum of the art of one world. The same trend is advancing in the universities, with special area studies on Africa, Asia, archaeology, anthropology. The universities are now living up to their name, and becoming universal.

Universalism is a fact. We live in a universe. Nature is one, and all its processes universal. We are a single species, and microbiology has proven to us that all creatures are members of a single family of life. Human culture is united in one cultural evolution. Only 10,000 years ago we were all in the Old Stone Age together, all hunters and gatherers, living in small bands. The making of stone tools was a world-wide art. There is but one scientific enterprise shared by all the world's peoples. The scientists shame our governments. Scientists from Russia and America collaborated in developing and proving the theory of the nuclear winter. An alliance of doctors against nuclear war has received the Nobel Peace Prize, and the organization is headed by a Soviet and an American physician. Universalism is the only way of thought and life that has any future, for all studies and research but further demonstrate its fundamental reality and wisdom.

The future of universal religion does not depend on a small denomination that professes it. Even if we did not practice it as poorly as we do, even if we realized it completely, it would not depend on us. It has permeated human thought and idealism. This we do know: if universalism does not have a future, then the human race has no future.

The future of the human venture depends on enough people becoming universal in their imagination, their learning, and their compassion. How many would be enough? Certainly they will have to be in positions of power and control. The Ayatollah Khomeni demonstrates how far we are from this, and how precarious our situation is. Lebanon is a disastrous object lesson of humanity divided by provincial, sectarian, and warring factions. With atomic weapons, we cannot survive another world war. The two world wars demonstrate the terrible price paid when universalism fails. A third would be fatal. If universalism has no future, we have no future.

Chapter 15

And Afterwards . . .

Maryell Cleary

The creative energy that Kenneth Patton brought to the Meeting House project faltered when he left in 1968; though the church went on with a new minister, its aims and programs changed. It was no longer the bold experiment of "a religion for one world" that it had been. By 1980 the Meeting House was officially closed and the building sold. The positive influence of the Meeting House, however, did not come to an end then. Indeed, it is still very much a living presence within Unitarian Universalism.

Parts of the project have been copied, more or less successfully. *A Religion for One World* shows photographs of the building for the First Unitarian Society in Schenectady, New York. It is a church in the round, designed by Edward Durrell Stone, and built during the ministry of William Gold. It has places for symbols inside and a sculpture garden out-of-doors. Presumably the building was modeled after the Meeting House, but later ministers and congregants know little about that original.

Some ministers have attempted to use elements of the Meeting House in their own buildings and services. UU minister Howard Box, now retired, reports that his efforts to include the great writings of world religions and cultures in one church's sanctuary met with teasing and belittling by some members of his congregation. They called it "book arranging" à la flower arranging. In another church he tried to have the symbols of the world religions placed on the sanctuary walls; this effort never got out of committee. However, for some time the UUA sold banners showing those symbols and many churches displayed them.

Some ministers and laypersons relate especially well to the emphasis on astronomy. As UU minister Susan Manker-Seale says, "I particularly like that the Meeting House put astronomy in the forefront with the mural of the galaxy. I use a poster, 'the birth of a star,' in some of my services." Susan also remarks on the creativity displayed in the Meeting House: "The Meeting House gave us a wonderful example of a creative faith; it was a story of hope for what we might do in our own churches. There's so much more to the world than one tradition." She also comments that the Meeting House gave her a comprehensive view of what our churches might be, bringing in art and beauty and mythology.

Without direct influence by the Meeting House or Ken Patton many liberal churches have included virtually every form of art in their buildings and services. Far from the Puritan tradition of bare walls and clear windows, today banners and weavings hang on walls, murals and stained glass tell our stories, sculptures and paintings enhance the meanings we choose. Although "the word" remains central, symbols—especially the flaming chalice—have become almost universal. And "the word" often includes something written by Ken Patton and first used in the Meeting House.

The bronze symbols representing many human activities now hang in the central room of the Starr King School for the Ministry. Professor Alicia McNary Forsey has told of their coming and their impact on the students in another part of this book. They are one tangible part of the Meeting House that lives on.

Hymns and readings written or arranged for use in the Meeting House appear in both *Hymns for the Celebration of Life* and the most recent hymnal, *Singing the Living Tradition*. A selection of Patton's writings for personal reflection and public reading may be found in the anthology *The Wonder Of Life* (Meeting House Press Revisited, 1997, edited by Maryell Cleary).

Robert Murphy, minister of the UU Fellowship of Falmouth, Massachusetts, writes, "People still ask, 'How will the liberal religions develop in the new age?' And I still say in response, 'Take a look at Ken

Patton's legacy and the story of the Charles Street Meeting House. Because Ken was anticipating our new century fifty years ago. Ken was the Universalist poet and the Humanist prophet who was exploring earth-based spirituality long before the first Earth Day.'" Murphy and others have found an environmentalist slant is much of Patton's work, particularly in the 1964 volume, *Man's Hidden Search*. It was published in the Meeting House years and, with the exception of the noninclusive language that was typical of the time, it is a classic of naturalistic mysticism. (It should be noted that Ken used gender-inclusive language in his later writings, revised many of his earlier works, and encouraged people using his texts to make appropriate changes.)

As liberal religion spreads, some of the emphasis the Meeting House put on other cultures and customs is turning up in other lands. Without direct connection with the Meeting House and not in response to anything in American Unitarian Universalism, UUs in other parts of the world just naturally add local elements in their worship.

Perhaps one day we may look back at the Meeting House and say, "See! It pointed the way!"

Contributors

(* Quoted in "And Afterwards . . .")

Howard Box*, Unitarian Universalist minister, Ethical Culture Leader; a founder and past president, Fellowship of Religious Humanists.

David Bumbaugh, Unitarian Universalist minister, Associate Professor of Ministry, Meadville/Lombard Theological School; author of *The Education of God* and *Unitarian Universalism: A Narrative History*.

Ernest Cassara, Professor Emeritus of History, George Mason University; editor of *Universalism in America*, author, *Hosea Ballou: The Challenge to orthodoxy*.

Maryell Cleary, Unitarian Universalist minister; editor, *The Wonder of Life* and *A Bold Experiment: The Charles Street Universalist Meeting House*.

Charlotte Sawyer Fish, Long-time active member of the Charles Street Universalist Meeting House.

Alicia McNary Forsey, Professor, Church History, Starr King School for the Ministry; Unitarian Universalist minister; Chair, UU Scholars Panel.

Charles A. Howe, Unitarian Universalist minister; editor, *Clarence R. Skinner: Prophet of a New Universalism*.

James A. Hunt, Unitarian Universalist minister; professor of religion; author of books about Gandhi.

Susan Manker-Seale*, Minister, Unitarian Universalist Congregation of Northwest Tucson; Graduate, Starr King School of the Ministry.

Robert F. Murphy*, Minister, Unitarian Universalist Fellowship of Falmouth, Massachusetts; environmental justice and human rights activist.

Kenneth L. Patton, Minister, Charles Street Meeting House, Unitarian Society of Ridgewood, New Jersey; author of *A Religion for One World* and other books.

Charles A. Reinhardt, Unitarian Universalist minister; "early admirer of the Ken Patton-Clint Scott Meeting House."

Paul Sawyer, Minister, Throop Memorial Unitarian Universalist Church, Pasadena, California; early member of the Meeting House.

Thomas Schade, Associate Minister, First Unitarian Church of Worcester, Massachusetts; member, Board of Directors, UU Christian Fellowship.

Peter Lee Scott, Unitarian Universalist minister; founding member of the Charles Street Meeting House.

Alan Seaburg, Curator of Manuscripts Emeritus, Harvard Divinity School (Harvard University); co-minister, Charles Street Meeting House, 1964–1968.